THE INCARNATION OF
AHRIMAN

Rudolf Joseph Lorenz Steiner
February 27, 1861 – March 30, 1925

FROM THE WORKS OF RUDOLF STEINER

THE INCARNATION OF
AHRIMAN

THE OCCULT ANNIHILATION OF THE SOUL

Dr. Douglas J. Gabriel

Our Spirit, LLC
2023

OUR SPIRIT, LLC
2023

P. O. Box 355
Northville, MI 48167

www.ourspirit.com
www.neoanthroposophy.com
www.gospelofsophia.com
www.eternalcurriculum.com

ISBN: 979-8-9864415-1-1 (paperback)
ISBN: 979-8-9864415-2-8 (e-book)

CONTENTS

Mechanical Occultism   55

The Incarnation
of Ahriman

We live in grave times. Reading the news headlines on any particular day, one can easily feel overwhelmed with the impending collapse of cultures, countries, financial markets, common decency, law and order, education, and spiritual and moral impulses. One crisis after another, whether real or false flag, is used to chisel away our personal freedoms and liberties, leading us into an Orwellian world of global governance and the complete annihilation of all that is divine in the world. We hold on to threadbare strands of hope, praying for mercy and divine intervention in a global quagmire that seems unsolvable.

Where is the messiah who was to come? Where is the path to Shamballa and Heaven? Where is the otherworldly exit from all this worldly madness? Are these the end days? Is this the Apocalypse?

If you are new to anthroposophy, you may not be aware that Rudolf Steiner spoke of these matters at great length. For those that have studied anthroposophy, you will recall that Steiner spoke of the "War of All against All", a time in the distant future that creates the transition to a "new heaven and a new Earth." What many may not be aware of is that this struggle can take place during any time-period, either in a microcosmic form or in a full-fledged battle between the light and dark.

To be victorious in this struggle, whether now or at the end of the seventh period, whether personally or globally—one must meet evil in its luciferic and ahrimanic forms with courage to see through their terrifying and daunting spectres of fear, hatred, and doubt; embracing in their place a spirit full of faith, hope, and love. To do so is to wield the sword of the Time Spirit, the Archai Michael, and slay the fiery dragon of untruthful materialism and selfish egoism. But first, one must become aware of evil, and like the miller's daughter in Rumpelstiltskin, call out his name in full recognition of the evil.

Dr. Rudolf Steiner wrote and lectured extensively on these beings—Lucifer and Ahriman—as well as the Being of Christ who incarnated in Palestine and is the second person in the Holy Trinity. What may be a surprise for readers new to Anthroposophy is that on each side of Christ there are two beings, a left-hand and right-hand path of evil. Those two beings of evil are Lucifer the tempter, the left-hand path of evil, and Ahriman the father of lies, the right-hand path of evil. Lucifer is the fallen Angelic being we know from the *Bible*. Ahriman, whose name is taken from Ancient Persia, where he was seen as the opposite of the Sun god Ahura Mazdao, is also known as Satan.

Another surprise comes from the teachings of Steiner that both Lucifer and Ahriman incarnate once as a human being in a physical body, Lucifer in approximately the Second Millennia BC and Ahriman in the Second Millennia AD, and that Christ balances their influences by incarnating in the middle through the body of Jesus of Nazareth. There is another being of evil that directly opposes Christ known as Sorat or Sorath, the Sun-Demon, who incarnates periodically from the realm of the Sun as an assault against the development of the human ego. He is often called the Anti-Christ. Sorat's physical incarnation is now being prepared by Ahriman and his helpers called Asuras. These four beings, Christ-Lucifer-Ahriman-Sorat, and their individual physical incarnations are part of the plan of spiritual evolution, and each being, even though deemed "evil", has important functions to contribute to the evolution of the free human being who must develop discernment to understand the difference between them. As hopeless as the world may seem at times, we can have comfort in knowing that the spirits of opposition are an important part of the Divine Plan.

Christ's incarnation created the "turning point of time" because all evolution revolves around this central event of human spiritual evolution. Christ incarnated only once to defeat the existing effects of Lucifer and his human incarnation in China and prepare humanity for the materialism of Ahriman and his human incarnation in North America. Christ conquers the delusional temptations of Lucifer just as He conquers the insidious lies of Ahriman by donating the form of the human ego (I Am) to humanity at the "turning point of time." Christ will also conquer Sorat's evil influence in the distant future when the Anti-Christ fully incarnates. Because of the deed of Christ through the Mystery of Golgotha, Christ's perfected ego now exists in an etheric form in the realm of the super-etheric (Shambala) that surrounds the living Earth. These perfected vehicles can replicate unendingly and are able to be used by those who can rise to their level of consciousness. Although it will take humanity quite some time to evolve into the use of the perfected vehicles of Christ consciousness, there are some advanced souls, and you may be one, who has accomplished this wonder and bring forth teachings that align with the living, perfected vehicles of Christ.

To become conscious of evil and help redeem it through Christ consciousness, we must know the many faces and manifestations of evil—the biographies of

Lucifer and Ahriman. We should understand the meaning of both Lucifer and Ahriman's physical incarnations and glean from that the wisdom to rise above their example of evil vices leading to the Seven Deadly Sins. The time has passed for recognizing the incarnations of Lucifer and Christ. We should have already learned what we needed from Lucifer's egotism and from Christ's selfless "I Am." Ahriman and Sorat are now leading humanity into a culture of Anti-Christ selfishness. Our immediate task today is to understand the anti-spiritual materialism of Ahriman and the physical incarnation of Ahriman who wishes to turn humans into transhuman automatons, non-thinking animals, and worse. No one has written more extensively about Ahriman than Rudolf Steiner, so it would seem only logical to read what he has written and said about the subject. The purpose of this book, *The Incarnation of Ahriman*, is to provide the aspirant and the initiate with a compilation of Steiner's descriptions of Ahriman and Lucifer, and where those descriptions are not easily quoted, provide the reader with a summation of Steiner's indications for each topic.

The Incarnations of Lucifer, Christ, Ahriman

The Ahrimanic Deception, Rudolf Steiner, Zurich, October 27, 1919, GA 193

"The impulses entering humanity from a luciferic source sank down gradually into the soul. The ahrimanic, is growing stronger and stronger in modern times. It will become increasingly strong in the near future and on into future ages. The ahrimanic impulse proceeds from a super-sensible Being different from the Being of Christ or of Lucifer. The influence of this Being becomes especially powerful in the fifth post-Atlantean epoch. If we look at the confused conditions of recent years, we shall find that men have been brought to such chaotic conditions mainly through the ahrimanic powers.

Just as there was an incarnation of Lucifer at the beginning of the third pre-Christian millennium, as there was the Christ Incarnation at the time of the Mystery of Golgotha, so there will be a Western incarnation of the Ahriman being in the third post-Christian millennium. At the one pole stands a luciferic incarnation, in the center, the incarnation of Christ, and at the other pole the ahrimanic incarnation. Lucifer is the power that stirs up in man all fanatical, all falsely mystical forces, all that physiologically tends to bring the blood into disorder and so lift man above and outside himself.

Ahriman is the power that makes man dry, prosaic, philistine—that ossifies him and brings him to the superstition of materialism. And the true nature and being of man is essentially the effort to hold the balance between the powers of Lucifer and Ahriman; the Christ Impulse helps present humanity to establish this equilibrium.

Viewed historically, we find that the luciferic preponderated in certain currents of cultural development of the pre-Christian age and continued into the first centuries of our era. On the other hand, the ahrimanic influence has been at work since the middle of the fifteenth century and will increase in strength until an actual incarnation of Ahriman takes place among Western humanity.

Ahrimanic powers prepare the evolution of mankind in such a way that it can fall a prey to Ahriman when he appears in human form within Western civilization as once Lucifer appeared in human form in China, as once Christ appeared in human form in Asia Minor. Ahriman will appear in human form and the only question is, how he will find humanity prepared. Will his preparations have secured for him as followers the whole of mankind that today calls itself civilized, or will he find a humanity that can offer resistance. Disregard of truth is precisely what will build Ahriman the best bridge to the success of his incarnation.

Ahriman stirs up all the emotions that split men up into small groups—groups that mutually attack one another. Ahriman also makes use of what develops from the old conditions of heredity which man has really outgrown in the fifth post-Atlantean epoch. The ahrimanic powers use all that is derived from old circumstances of heredity in order to set men against each other in conflicting groups. All that comes from old differences of family, race, tribe, peoples, is used by Ahriman to create confusion.

Ahriman skilfully prepares his goal beforehand; ever since the Reformation and the Renaissance, the economist has been emerging in modern civilization as the representative governing type. Since that time the economist has been in command. Rulers are in fact merely the handymen, the under strappers of the economists.

We know very well that we have no occasion either to hate Ahriman or to fear Lucifer, since their powers are inimical only when they are working outside the realm where they belong. Luciferic activity has the result of making the will young. When the activity of our soul is streamed through by luciferic activity the result is will. When the luciferic influence predominates, when Lucifer makes his forces felt in the soul, then will is active in us. Lucifer has a rejuvenating influence on the whole stream of our soul-activity.

When Ahriman brings his influence to bear on our soul-activity, he hardens it, it becomes old, and thinking is the result. The etheric body actually has this appearance; one can perceive in it luciferic light and ahrimanic hardness. But there are places where the etheric body seems to be quite non-transparent, as if it had ice tracings in it. This freezing of the etheric body at certain places is due to Ahriman; his forces have found entry there by means of thought. There are also places which seem to be full of light. Here the etheric body is transparent and gleams and glows with light. It is Lucifer who sends his rays into the etheric body of man and makes the centers of will. Then there are regions in between, where the etheric body is in perpetual movement and activity. Here you see at one moment hardness—and then suddenly the hardness is caught by a ray of light and melts right away. Hardening and dissolving, in perpetual alternation—such is the expression of the activity of feeling in the etheric body.

When the ahrimanic forces gain the upper hand, we have an expression of thinking; when the luciferic forces are in ascendance, we have an expression of willing; and when they are in mutual conflict one with the other, we have an expression of feeling.

Ahriman has great power over our waking consciousness. In sleep consciousness, Lucifer has the upper hand. They are in equilibrium only when we dream; there they pull with equal force, they strike a balance between them. The ideas which are called forth by Ahriman in day consciousness and which he causes to harden and crystallize are dissolved and made to disappear under the influence of Lucifer.

Thus, we are truly, in a certain connection, redeemers of Lucifer. When we begin to be able to love our duty, then the moment has come when we can help towards the redemption and release of the luciferic powers; we set free the Lucifer forces which are held in us as by a charm and lead them forth to fight with Ahriman. We release the imprisoned Lucifer (imprisoned in self-love) when we learn to love our duty.

Calm and peace of mind have the coldness of Ahriman; in the quiet understanding of what is in the world, we unite our warmth and our understanding love with the coldness that is in the world outside. And then we release Ahriman, when we meet what has come about with understanding, when we do not merely demand our rights out of self-love but understand what has come about in the world. In the revolutionary stream lives Lucifer, in the conservative stream Ahriman, and man in his life of right lives in the midst between these two poles. This is the eternal battle that is waged between Lucifer and Ahriman."

Ahriman and Lucifer in the Modern World

In the modern world, ahrimanic shadow-thoughts rule the day. Our media devices are so alluring and addictive that children and adults seldom turn away from them for long. Whether those platforms are television, smart phones, game systems, computers, or virtual reality, they are seductive distractions that draw our attention away from the invisible spiritual to the materialism of an electronic world where Ahriman ensnares us in his spider web network of grey shadow thoughts. The ego of the unwitting devotee of Ahriman is entangled in Facebook, Twitter, Instagram, and a plethora of electronic prisons that fabricate a false version of the human ego—a digital-ego that "appears" to be connected with other human egos, but is, in fact, a complete mirage of one's true ego.

Any of us can appear to be clever as we access unlimited information from search engines, but this is hardly having knowledge that is earned by rigorous thinking and actual experience. Ahriman gives us the illusion of having all knowledge at our fingertips, but what we really have is so much information that we are overwhelmed with indigestible digital nonsense. It is hard to discern the pearls from the swill. In fact, Ahriman uses the ease of posting information on a digital platform to confuse us even more. An entire world of anti-knowledge and propaganda fills the digital world, drowning us in so much information that it is difficult to discern truth from fiction. Fake websites, false-flag events, photo-shopped images, propaganda, lies, deceit, and distractions continue to pour into the great fathom of the internet which is as unlimited as our Cosmos. Ahriman's intent of destroying human intelligence and diverting us from the pursuit of spiritual consciousness is accomplished when we are so overwhelmed by the digital world that we simply become unconsciously absorbed in its electronic energy. Sadly, many of us don't have the consciousness to know that this has already happened and any thought of spiritual beings and a world outside of materialism is not even considered.

An over-reaction to the influence of Ahriman might be to eschew all electronic platforms and anything that smacks of materialism. But Ahriman would not be in the world if he didn't have something to offer the initiate for spiritual evolution. Just as Lucifer gave man the capacity of thinking, Ahriman will give man the sacred magic of willpower. It behoves the initiate to recognize Ahriman as he manifests in the world today so that his incarnation can be redeemed for a higher purpose in man.

The higher spiritual forces of Christ, the middle-path, can discern the good and ill that both Lucifer and Ahriman offer to the human soul at every moment of decision. There is no ultimate evil, just regressive beings who resist the progressive beings. These beings of evil will be redeemed in time, but the soul of the individual is in the middle of a pitched battle for its ego. Lucifer would have us ascend into the spiritual world too quickly and Ahriman would have us forget our spiritual nature and be forever imprisoned in materialism.

Luciferic beings are regressive spiritual beings. There have been regressive beings involved in each of the planetary incarnations of Earth—Old Saturn, Old Sun, Old Moon, and Earth. Each set of regressive beings has a separate name and somewhat different ways of manifesting. The regressive beings of the Old Moon incarnation of Earth are called luciferic and are found working in the astral body (desire body) of human beings. The regressive beings of the Old Sun incarnation of Earth are called ahrimanic and are found working in the etheric body (life body) of the human being. The regressive beings of the Old Saturn incarnation of Earth are called asuric and work through the physical body of the human being.

In the astral body of the human being, the luciferic beings try to draw humanity away from the normal Earth evolution to their own realms of light—an illusion. In the human soul, they inspire pride, egotism, disinterest in others, fiery emotionalism, subjectivity, fantasy, and hallucinations. In the human intellect, luciferic beings inspire generalization, unification, hypothesizing, and the building of imaginative, fantastical pictures that are beyond reality. Human speech and thought were given by luciferic beings to humanity, which eventually developed into self-consciousness and the capacity for independent thinking.

When Lucifer incarnated in a human body, he brought about a revolution in human consciousness. Before then, humanity could not use the organs of intellect and lived by a kind of instinct. Lucifer, as a spiritual being and as a human being, was the first to comprehend through the human intellect the wisdom of the mystery schools. The effects of Lucifer's incarnation inspired culture from the times of the ancient Chinese, all the way through to the teachings of the Gnostics, even lingering into the early nineteenth century. The great initiates took it upon themselves to enter into the luciferic realms and turn them towards the benefit of mankind. Only through the luciferic influence has mankind risen above the status of immaturity and instinctual awareness into the realm of an independent and free thinker. Ahriman, too, has his purpose for helping man evolve as this biography of Ahriman will illustrate.

Lucifer, Christ, and Ahriman

Thinking and Willing as Two Poles of the Human Soul-Life, Rudolf Steiner, Dornach, July 15, 1921, GA 205

"Thus, our life is poised mid-way between the annihilation of Earthly existence and the building up of Earthly existence, in other words, between Lucifer and Ahriman. Lucifer is concerned with the attempt to make us into non-corporeal beings; he would fain lift us right out of Earthly existence. Lucifer, if he could, would spiritualise us, or shall we say de-materialize us. But Ahriman is his opponent. Ahriman works in such a way that he continually fills in what is hollowed out by Lucifer. If you wished to give plastic expression to Lucifer and Ahriman you could do it very well by merging your material in such a way that the figure of Ahriman was continually pressing into the hollows and curves of Lucifer, as though desirous of turning him inside out. And because these hollows and cavities are actually present within us, they must be pushed outwards, they must, as it were, be turned inside out. Ahriman and Lucifer are two opposing forces, and both work in the human being. Equilibrium lies between them. The result of Lucifer's persistent efforts at dematerialization is: Materialization. When we perceive: Lucifer. When we think over that which we have perceived: Ahriman. When we form ideas with regard to our desires and wishes: Lucifer. When we really bring our will-forces into play on the Earth: Ahriman. Thus, we stand midway between them both. As human beings we are placed in the most intimate relationship with the ahrimanic and luciferic powers, and we learn to understand man only when we consider him in connection with these polar-opposites. Christ stands there as the Balance between Lucifer and Ahriman."

Ahriman Takes a Human Body

The being of Ahriman will use all aspects of scientific materialism to bring a form of mechanical occultism and fake clairvoyance to his followers. He will appear as a type of anti-Christ who his disciples will believe to be another incarnation of Christ. There will be no love in Ahriman and his cold heart will not be able to help freedom and love develop, only fear and hatred. Christ will antidote this evil by appearing in the etheric realm in what is commonly called the "second coming of Christ in the etheric." This etheric clairvoyance will be the opposite of the mechanical occultism clairvoyance which Ahriman will grant his followers. Ahriman's clairvoyance will lead to dead ends and will not help the aspirant advance to the astral-light vision of Christ in the etheric realm.

Ahriman's followers will have different visions that will not coincide with one another. Instead of connecting humans to one another and to divine beings, Ahriman separates humans from each other and anything spiritual. When you see a world divided into countless factions, battling one another with angry words or devastating wars, you see the manifestation of Ahriman. Basically, this is a pre-figuring of the apocalyptic "War of All against All" that will come in the distant future, or, if we don't become spiritually vigilant, may come to pass in our time.

Ahriman has been working to steal human intelligence since printing was invented. The printed word, book, or library gives the reader the illusion that the knowledge in print, the book in his hand, is his personal knowledge. This concept explodes infinitely with the invention of the Internet, giving any user information about history, cultures, or any subject. It takes spiritual work and effort to embody knowledge, as any ardent student of Steiner will attest. Knowledge is not obtained by surfing, clicking, and scanning web pages. Knowledge must ripen with time and grow into wisdom before it is infused by Christ with love in the free human soul and spirit.

Ahriman amplifies information to the point that anything of spiritual value is muted. He then has been effective in keeping humanity from knowing its spiritual origins and future. This conflagration of digital information may provide endless knowledge, but without the integration of human warmth, it will not be imbued with wisdom. Ahriman and Lucifer will give us plenty of information and cleverness, but without Christ, knowledge cannot yield wisdom.

Anthroposophically speaking, Ahriman is a retarded or regressive hierarchical spiritual being of the rank of the Spirits of Form from the Old Sun incarnation of Earth. He works in the realm of the Archai (Spirits of Time) and can be found active in the etheric body of the human being. Ahriman's ultimate intent is to foil the goals of human spiritual evolution.

Ahriman and his hosts wish to freeze the Earth into complete rigidity, so that it will not pass over to the Future Jupiter, Future Venus, and Future Vulcan incarnations of Earth, and to make the human being into an entirely Earthly being who is not individualized, a slave to materialism, who is divorced from the divine. He wants to materialize, crystallize, darken, silence, and kill the living spirit. Ahriman promotes the illusion, the lie, that matter is primary reality, or the only reality. Ahriman's lies and untruthfulness are a delusion in time that will one day dissolve.

The modern scientific revolution, since the fifteenth century, has been inspired largely by Ahriman. He is the inspirer of amoral, atheistic, mechanistic materialism. He wants humanity to live from unconscious instincts as a member of a collective herd. Ahriman teaches that humanity is derived from animals and is little better.

Scientific materialistic thinking is hardly conscious or comprehensive. Each scientific area is a silo of its own, rarely exploring fields afar or integrating whole living processes in its investigations. Ahriman wants humanity to be part of a herd, a general species of pseudo-humans who are clever, Earth-bound animals that experience the world through narrow vision and are not conscious of their life beyond the borders of birth and death.

Ahriman believes there is no spirit or soul in the world but that life itself is a mechanical process, a machine of sorts. He is more apt to liken the body to a machine than to an Angel. He works through subconscious instincts inspiring fear, hatred, lust for power, and destructive sex impulses. He inspires rigid, automatic thinking that is hard and literal, not soaring and imaginative.

Ahriman uses hollow words to separate language from meaning and reality. Language becomes dead under his rulership and human warmth is withdrawn from conversation. Eventually, ahrimanic thinking leads us to thoughts devoid of spirit. Only by consciously imbuing our thoughts, conversations, and writings with human warmth are we able to counter the death of spirit in our language.

Another tendency of ahrimanic thinking is nationalism based on ethnicity with dogmatic party politics breeding hatred for others, destroying cultural, political, and economic life. Ahriman promotes mechanization of the world bound by rigid laws everywhere, with little place for free human initiative. Philistinism, tedium, alienation, and lack of interest in one's work kill human intelligence and imagination.

In medicine, we find Ahriman entrenched in materialistic, mechanistic experimentalism and treatment, isolating symptoms of the patient from his whole physical health and environment in order to prescribe federally approved allopathic drugs that better serve pharmaceutical companies rather than the patient. The ahrimanic cycle of the medical industry is quite disturbing. First poison the crops with irradiation, pesticides, and genetically modified foods all in the name of growing better harvests, which, in turn, cause disease and illness, which then creates a life-long customer for the medical industry.

To serve Ahriman you can vaccinate a child with massive inoculations, causing medical conditions immediately or in the future, and create another steady customer base for the medical tyrants. Then, process and pasteurize foods so that they are left without enzymes and are indigestible, causing further symptoms that create even more customers. Create a medical system so that every symptom can be checked off an extensive list which has a corresponding government approved drug to treat the symptom. Punish any doctor that goes outside of these parameters because holistic approaches to healing do not bring repeat customers to medical big business. Make sure alternative remedies are discouraged or outlawed by regulation or legislation. Then, when humanity is too ill to think about the spiritual world, Ahriman will rule the human body.

This is an example of how Ahriman works in the world of money, power, greed, and the severance of man from his spiritual source until a human is nothing more than a cog in a medical industry wheel, our physical bodies used as economic food for others to feed upon. Similar analogies could be given for big business involved in education, war, politics, and organized religion.

For example, ahrimanic materialistic interpretations of the Gospels make Christ into a simple man with little spiritual connection to the modern human. Worship of the physical world leads humans to deny life after death and therefore to a struggle to find solace exclusively in the physical world. Once Ahriman closes off the spiritual world to humans, they can easily lose connection to morality, spirituality, and a virtuous life. Instead, they begin a descent towards a more animal-like existence, spiralling downward through the seven deadly sins.

Instead of "feeding the gods" with our Christened etherized blood, we feed Ahriman with physical bodies that have become diseased by Ahriman's own mechanical processes that sabotage health, healing, and spiritual evolution. Instead of partaking in a reciprocal stream of spiritual nutrition between humans and Angels that lift us into higher dimensions of consciousness, we are tethered to an ahrimanic stream which binds us in a material prison that keeps us from knowing our spiritual past or future.

Ahriman hardens the etheric body in man so that it becomes a vehicle of automatic, intellectual thinking devoid of will, permanently shackling human etheric bodies to the region immediately surrounding the Earth after death. This is the realm of "hungry ghosts", as described in Tibetan Buddhism. Man would become clever, animalistic, ghostly, Earth-bound creatures under Ahriman's guidance. The Earth would become so hardened without the vibrancy of human etheric bodies that it could not pass over to the Future Jupiter incarnation of Earth. Ahriman's followers seek a kind of "immortality" in the slag-Earth that will surround the Earth with Old Moon forces. It will be an immortality with egotistic, Earth-bound consciousness instead of the cosmic consciousness of the individualized spiritual ego. The old Earth would be preserved, and parts of humanity would become etheric and astral ghosts, imprisoned in bodies made of Earth substance that does not dissolve. Those animal-humans would not be able to ascend to spiritual heights but would remain chained to Earth as egoless soul-beings. Ahriman will preserve materialistic dead thinking through a condensed etheric body of the Earth in the realms between the Earth and the Moon. In doing so, Ahriman darkens the etheric realm where Christ can be found and instead promises an ahrimanic immortality in the hell realms—the Eighth Sphere.

Despite these ominous descriptions of Ahriman, his incarnation need not be the end of the world. His incarnation is necessary in human and Earthly evolution and can be turned towards the good if humanity meets it in the right way. Ahriman wants us to be unconscious; but it is our responsibility to strive to be more and more conscious, and to help inculcate consciousness in as many people as we can. We can become more aware of the meaning of our own lives and of the world by studying and filling ourselves with the modern form of cosmic wisdom given by spiritual science. Just as the ancient initiates entered into luciferic wisdom and rescued it for the good of mankind; now mankind must, with the consciousness gained from spiritual science and from the Etheric Christ, enter into ahrimanic knowledge and turn it to good uses.

Ahrimanic knowledge will show what cleverness can, and cannot, produce from Earthly forces. If we meet Ahriman consciously, we can acquire through him the realization that the Earth is becoming old and must decline physically, eventually to die and enter the spiritual worlds, to be reborn as the Future Jupiter incarnation of Earth. Ahriman wishes to preserve, condense, and harden the old Earth and its etheric body so that it will not evolve into the Future Jupiter incarnation of Earth but will become a dwelling place for his beings, a new planet of his own making—the Eighth Sphere.

Ahriman is the false prince of the world who makes the claim that he is the one who guides and leads humanity. He is the mighty teacher of materialistic Darwinism and technology. His goal is to slay human awareness of spirituality in us and harden the ego. Ahriman wants to create a humanity that is a group soul of animals which thinks without using the vehicle of an ego, or human I consciousness. He tries to numb us to the fact that humans have the capacity to think Angelic thoughts, spiritual thoughts. Whereas Christ wishes to create a new spiritual Earth from the old one through love and human freedom, Ahriman wants to destroy the cosmic plan and be the god of his own world.

Ahriman's Incarnation in the West

The Influences of Lucifer and Ahriman, Human Responsibility for the Earth, Rudolf Steiner, Dornach, 1919, GA 191

"Just as there was an incarnation of Lucifer in the flesh and an incarnation of Christ in the flesh, so, before only a part of the third millennium of the post-Christian era has elapsed, there will be, in the West, an actual incarnation of Ahriman: Ahriman in the flesh. But what matters is that people shall find the right vantage point from which to confront it. If Ahriman were able to slink into a humanity unaware of his coming, that would gladden him most of all.

Ahriman's impulse is clearly evident in the spread of the belief that the mechanistic, mathematical conceptions inaugurated by Galileo, Copernicus, and others, explain what is happening in the Cosmos. The Cosmos is permeated by soul and spirit. It is this knowledge that Ahriman, in preparing his Earthly incarnation, wants to withhold. Whatever can separate people into groups, whatever can alienate them from mutual understanding the whole world over and drive wedges between them, strengthens Ahriman's impulse.

It was a pre-eminently luciferic culture that persisted until after the Mystery of Golgotha—a culture inspired by the incarnation of Lucifer in China in the third millennium B.C. Many influences of this incarnation continued to radiate and were still powerful in the early Christian centuries; indeed, they are working to this day. Through Lucifer, human beings have acquired the faculty of using the organs of their intellect, of their power of intellectual discernment. It was Lucifer himself, in a human body, who was the first to grasp through the power of intellect what formerly could be imparted to humanity only through revelation, namely, the content of the Mysteries.

But now that we are facing an incarnation of Ahriman in the third millennium after Christ, Lucifer's tracks are becoming less visible, and Ahriman's activities in such trends as I have indicated are coming into prominence. The ahrimanic incarnation will be greatly furthered if people fail to establish a free and independent spiritual life and allow it to remain entangled in the economic or political life. To the ahrimanic power a free spiritual life would denote a kind of darkness, and people's interest in it, a burning, raging fire.

It should be realized that just as external science becomes ahrimanic, the higher development of our inner nature becomes luciferic if we give ourselves up to mystical experiences. There is nothing more ahrimanic than this knowledge of the material world, for it is sheer illusion. Nevertheless, if the fata morgana that arises out of chemistry, out of physics, out of astronomy and the like can fill us with fiery enthusiasm and interest, then through our interest—which is itself luciferic—we can take from Ahriman what is his own. Nothing does more to prepare the path for Ahriman's incarnation than to find this or that tedious, to consider oneself superior to one thing or another and refuse to enter into it.

The incarnation of Ahriman in human form may be able to mislead and corrupt humankind on Earth to the uttermost. A task of humankind during the next phase of civilization will be to live toward the incarnation of Ahriman with such alert consciousness that this incarnation can serve to promote a higher, spiritual development, inasmuch as through Ahriman himself humanity will become aware of what can, or shall we say, cannot be achieved by physical life alone.

It must be realized that Ahriman will live among people on the Earth, but that in confronting him people will themselves determine what they may learn from him, what they may receive from him. This, however, they will not be able to do unless, from now onward, they take control of certain spiritual and also unspiritual currents which otherwise are used by Ahriman for the purpose of leaving humankind as deeply unconscious as possible of his coming; then, one day, he will be able to appear on Earth and overwhelm people tempting and luring them to repudiate Earth evolution, thus preventing it from reaching its goal.

In the future people will either receive spiritual knowledge consciously or consume the spirit unconsciously, thereby delivering it into the hands of the luciferic powers. This stream of spirit-and-soul-consumption is particularly encouraged by Ahriman because in this way he can lull humankind into greater and greater drowsiness, so that then, through his incarnation, he will be able to come among people and fall upon them unawares because they do not confront him consciously.

Everything that is developing as intellectual life without being suffused by warmth of soul, without being quickened by enthusiasm, directly furthers the incarnation of Ahriman in a way that is after his own heart. It lulls people to sleep. Chauvinism, perverted patriotism in every form—this is the material from which Ahriman will build just what he needs.

And those who believe they are being most truly Christian by rejecting any development of the conception of the Christ mystery, are, in their arrogance, the ones who do most to promote Ahriman's aims. The denominations and sects are positively spheres of encouragement, breeding-grounds for Ahriman. Just as the materialistic attitude, rejecting the spiritual altogether and contending that the human being is a product of what people eat and drink, furthers Ahriman's aims, so are these aims furthered by the stubborn rejection of everything spiritual and adherence to the literal, "simple" conception of the Gospels. In their day, the Gospels were given as a necessary counterweight to the luciferic gnosis; but if no attempt is made to develop understanding of their content, the aims of Ahriman are furthered, not the progress of humankind.

If, in the future, people were to do nothing themselves toward acquiring a new wisdom, then, without their consciousness, the whole of culture would become ahrimanic, and it would be easy for the influences issuing from Ahriman's incarnation to permeate all civilization on the Earth. Through certain stupendous acts he would bring to humanity all the clairvoyant knowledge which until then can be acquired only by dint of intense labour and effort. When Ahriman incarnates in the West at the appointed time, he would establish a great occult school for the practice of magic arts of the greatest grandeur, and what otherwise can be acquired only by strenuous effort would be poured over humankind. The clairvoyance of each individual will be strictly differentiated. What one person would see, a second and a third would not see. Human beings would succumb to Ahriman simply through not having acquired by their own efforts what Ahriman is ready and able to give them. The result would be the establishment of Ahriman's kingdom on Earth and the overthrow of everything achieved hitherto by human culture.

Our concern is that the wisdom of the future—a clairvoyant wisdom—shall be rescued from the clutches of Ahriman. Again, let it be repeated that there is only one book of wisdom, not two kinds of wisdom. The issue is whether this wisdom is in the hands of Ahriman or of Christ.

A good way of playing into Ahriman's hands is to exclude everything of the nature of knowledge from denominational religion and to insist that simple faith is enough. If people cling to this simple faith, they condemn their soul to stagnation and then the wisdom that must be rescued from Ahriman cannot find entry. The root of the matter is that for the wisdom of the future too, a struggle is necessary, a struggle like that waged against Lucifer by the ancient initiates through whose intermediary the faculties of speech and of thinking were transmitted to humanity. Just as it devolved upon the initiates of the primeval wisdom to wrest from Lucifer that which has become human reason, human intellect, so the insight which is to develop in the future into the inner realities of things must be wrested from the ahrimanic powers.

We have only to remember that it is the endeavour of the ahrimanic powers to reduce the Earth to a state of complete rigidification. Their victory would be won if they succeeded in bringing Earth, water, and air into this rigidified state. Were that to happen, the Earth could not again acquire the Saturn warmth from which it proceeded, and which must be regained in the Vulcan epoch; and to prevent this is the aim of the ahrimanic powers. It must be realized that in very truth the human being is balanced as it were between the luciferic and the ahrimanic powers, and that the Christ has become a companion of human beings, leading them, first away from the battle with Lucifer, and then into the battle with Ahriman."

Ahriman's Incarnation in the West

The Cosmic New Year, The Mystery of the Human Will,
Rudolf Steiner, Lecture III, December 29, 1919, GA 195

"When the incarnation of Ahriman takes place in the Western World we shall simply see inscribed in the local Register, the birth of John William Smith (of course, this will not be the name) and people will look upon the child as a citizen in comfortable circumstances like any other, and they will sleep through what has, in reality, taken place.

You must realize that there is no better way to prepare for the fact that Ahriman is endeavouring cunningly to capture the whole Earth for his evolution, than that man should continue to live an abstract life, steeping himself in abstractions, as he does in the social life of today. This is one of the ruses, one of the clever tricks, by which Ahriman prepares in his own way for his lordship over the Earth.

There is also another form of preparation for Ahriman which can happen through an erroneous view of the Gospels. The conception of the Gospels has gradually become completely materialized. It is of the most extreme importance to Ahriman so to prepare his incarnation that through Spiritual Science man shall not follow this path of Imagination in the Gospels on to the Reality of the Mystery of Golgotha. The incarnation of Ahriman, in a future not very far distant, can be helped on its way just as well by an obscured worship of the Gospels as by abstract thinking."

Sorat and the Asuras

The Asuras remained behind in the Old Saturn incarnation of Earth and now work as regressive Archai (Time Spirits) who long to destroy the human ego, or "I consciousness." The Asuras work with the Sun-Demon Sorat (Sorath). Sorat is the Apocalyptic Beast 666 who also works with all ahrimanic forces and beings. If we identify the Anti-Christ of the Apocalypse as Sorat, we can picture Lucifer and Ahriman as the left and right hands of Sorat. Christ strives to hold Lucifer and Ahriman in balance so that they serve the good, while Sorat strives to keep them out of balance, so that they work towards destruction. The Asuras seek to destroy the ego itself, along with the Earth.

The aims of the Western occult circles not only relate to the spiritual imprisoning of humanity but ultimately to the endeavour to put the whole undertaking into the service of Sorat, who is the prime opponent of the ego principle in humanity. The overwhelming of humanity through artificial intelligence that has come about will lead ultimately to the loss of the ego.

The ahrimanic powers serving Sorat work in tandem with this intent, especially since 1998 (3 x 666). Ahriman makes use of the forces of sub-nature to penetrate "Michaelic Intelligence" (Cosmic Wisdom) with the artificial machine intelligence created by him, which includes the digitization of thought and the illusion of virtual reality. This dehumanizing process started with the deadening of human thoughts through the process of printing and continues now through multimedia digitization. The question becomes one of whether the human being controls the computer and the ahrimanic spider web of the Internet, or whether they control the human being.

Ahriman and the Asuras

The Deed of Christ and the Opposing Spiritual Powers, Lucifer, Ahriman, Asuras, Rudolf Steiner, January 1, 1909, GA 107

"In the Lemurian epoch it was the luciferic beings who intervened in man's evolution, in opposition to the Powers who at that time were striving to help him forward. In the Atlantean epoch, the Spirits opposing the progressive Powers were the Spirits of "Ahriman" or "Mephistopheles." The ahrimanic or Mephistophelean spirits—to give the precise names—are those known in medieval times as the Spirits of "Satan"—who must not be confused with "Lucifer."

The host of ahrimanic spirits has worked upon man since the middle of the Atlantean epoch onwards. They enticed him into regarding everything in his environment as material, with the result that he does not see through this material world to its true, spiritual foundations. Were man to have perceived the Spiritual in every stone, in every plant, in every animal, he would never have fallen into error and therewith into evil. Karma was thus the indirect consequence of the deeds of Ahriman.

It was in the second soul-member, the intellectual soul—the transformed part of the ether-body—that Ahriman established his footing. From there he lures humanity to false conceptions and judgments of material things, leads them to error, to sin, to lying—to everything that originates in the intellectual or mind soul. In every illusion that matter is the sole reality, we must perceive the whispered promptings of Ahriman, of Mephistopheles.

In the course of the Earth-period, man will cast away all the evil brought to him by the luciferic spirits together with the blessing of freedom. The evil brought by the ahrimanic spirits can be shed in the course of karma. But the evil brought by the asuric powers cannot be expunged in this way. Whereas the good Spirits instituted pain and suffering, illness, and death in order that despite the possibility of evil, man's evolution may still advance, whereas the good Spirits made possible the working of karma to the end that the ahrimanic powers might be resisted and the evil made good, it will not be so easy to counter the asuric powers as Earth-existence takes its course. For these asuric spirits will prompt what has been seized hold of by them, namely the very core of man's being, the Consciousness Soul together with the 'I', to unite with Earthly materiality. Fragment after fragment will be torn out of the 'I', and in the same measure in which the asuric spirits establish themselves in the consciousness soul, man must leave parts of his existence behind on the Earth. What thus becomes the prey of the asuric powers will be irretrievably lost. Not that the whole man need become their victim—but parts of his spirit will be torn away by the asuric powers.

These asuric powers are heralded today by the prevailing tendency to live wholly in the material world and to be oblivious of the realty of spiritual beings and spiritual worlds. True, the asuric powers corrupt man today in a way that is more theoretical than actual. Today, they deceive him by various means into thinking that his 'I' is a product of the physical world only; they lure him to a kind of theoretic materialism. But as time goes on—and the premonitory signs of this are the dissolute, sensuous passions that are becoming increasingly prevalent on Earth—they will blind man's vision of the spiritual Beings and spiritual Powers. Man will know nothing nor desire to know anything of a spiritual world. More and more he will not only teach that the highest moral ideals of humanity are merely sublimations of animal impulses, that human thinking is but a transformation of a faculty also possessed by the animals, that man is akin to the animal in respect of his form and moreover in his whole being descends from the animal—but he will take this view in all earnestness and order his life in accordance with it."

The Beginning of Ahriman's Efforts

The Principle of Spiritual Economy, Results of Spiritual Scientific Investigations of the Evolution of Humanity, Rudolf Steiner, Lecture IV, Rome, March 28, 1909, GA 109

"According to the divine plan, human beings were not supposed to perceive the world with external sense organs before the middle of the Atlantean period, but the luciferic forces made this happen earlier, at a time when human instincts had not yet matured. That represents the "Fall" of mankind. Religious documents tell us that the snake opened man's eyes, but without the interference of Lucifer the human body would not have become as firm as it now is and the Atlantean humanity would have been able to see the spiritual side of all things. Instead, man fell into sin, illusion, and error, and to make things worse, toward the middle of the Atlantean period he was also subjected to the influence of ahrimanic forces. The luciferic forces had worked on the astral body, but the ahrimanic forces worked on the etheric body, especially on the ether-head. By that, many human beings fell into the error of mistaking the physical world for the world of truth. The name "ahrimanic" comes from Ahriman, the name the Persians gave to this erroneous principle. Ahriman is identical with Mephistopheles and has nothing to do with Lucifer. Satan in the Bible is Ahriman too, not Lucifer.

Although the ahrimanic influence began in the Atlantean epoch, as we have said, it unfolded its full strength only later in human evolution. The ancient Indians were sufficiently protected against Ahriman; for them the physical world was never anything else but maya, illusion. Only in the most ancient Persian period of Zarathustra did people begin to place value on the physical world and thereby come into the power of Ahriman."

Lucifer and Ahriman during Atlantis and Post-Atlantean Times

Memory and Habit, The Sense for Truth, The Phenomenon of Metamorphosis in Life, Rudolf Steiner, Dornach, Lecture I August 26, 1916, GA 170

"The moment a luciferic activity sets in, the other side of the balance begins to operate: the ahrimanic impulse. While on the one side we memorise, calling Lucifer to our aid in this respect, on the other side we make more and more use of the ahrimanic support to memory, namely, we write things down. I have often said that it was a true conception in the Middle Ages which made men speak of printing as one of the 'black arts.'

Man's task is to cultivate the position of balance and not to believe that he can simply escape from the clutches of Lucifer and Ahriman. Calmly and courageously, he must admit to himself that both beings are necessary for world-evolution, that in his own development he needs both Lucifer and Ahriman in his active life, but that the balance must be maintained in every sphere of life.

At the beginning of the *Old Testament* there is a significant picture of the influx of the luciferic forces into world-evolution. Luciferic forces enter Earthly evolution by way of the woman. This biblical picture symbolises the influx of the luciferic element which occurred in the age of old Lemuria.

Then, during the subsequent Atlantean age, there came the entrance of the ahrimanic element into Earthly evolution. Just as during the fourth Post-Atlantean period human knowledge had to come to an understanding of the luciferic symbol, so now, during our fifth post-Atlantean epoch, it was necessary to place before the soul the opposite symbol. The figure of Faust has Ahriman at his side, as Eve has Lucifer. Lucifer approaches the woman, Eve; Ahriman approaches the man, Faust. And just as the man, Adam, was indirectly beguiled through Eve, so here, the woman, Gretchen, is deceived through the man, Faust. The seduction of Gretchen is the result of deception because Ahriman is at work. Ahriman is the 'Lying Spirit' in contrast to Lucifer who is the 'Tempter.'

Much exists in the world for the express purpose of guarding mankind from temptation by Lucifer: rules of conduct, maxims, moral precepts, instituted customs and so forth. But there is less to help man to protect himself in the right way from falling prey to the ahrimanic impulse—namely, untruthfulness.

All that is luciferic in man has to do with the emotions, the passions. On the other hand, the ahrimanic influence which asserts itself in human evolution has to do with lying, with untruthfulness. Ahriman feels a certain satisfaction on account of the evil that is in the world. We must acquire the power to conquer Ahriman within us at every moment."

Ahriman Throughout History

The Challenge of the Times, Rudolf Steiner, Dornach, November 29, 1918, GA 189

"When we look at the period of human evolution when mankind was approaching the Mystery of Golgotha, we find that the state of equilibrium between the luciferic and the ahrimanic forces was extraordinarily fluctuating, vacillating—no real balance was there. We have on one hand the stream of mankind which is moving towards the Mystery of Golgotha and manifests historically in the evolution of the Semitic peoples. This stream is particularly susceptible to the luciferic influence, whereby a strong ahrimanic activity is brought about in the subconscious.

On the other hand, the Greek nature is highly susceptible to the forces of Ahriman, and this brings about great luciferic activity in the subconscious. We can fully understand the Semitic and Greek cultures—polaric opposites of one another—only by keeping in mind this vacillation in human evolution between the ahrimanic and the luciferic. Precisely through the ahrimanic intervention experienced by the Greeks, and manifest as a luciferic element of their art, they had developed a lofty wisdom. And this wisdom took on a very individual, humanly individual, character. But fundamentally it was at its greatest where there still shone into it out of primeval times the teachings received from actual spiritual beings.

This ancient knowledge of man, however, was mediated by way of Lucifer, and men worked upon it with the aid of ahrimanic forces. Now at the time when the ancient world was passing away and from the other side came the Mystery of Golgotha, the ahrimanic forces began to gain a slight ascendancy; they were then particularly strong. And since the sixteenth century something similar is happening again—a kind of renaissance of the ahrimanic forces. And through them man's life of soul was driven in the direction of the abstract—towards that abstraction which meets us in the thoroughly abstract nature of the Romans.

Through the incursion of the Mystery of Golgotha men were given from spiritual heights, which were no longer within their reach on Earth, a renewed capacity for grasping themselves as persons. The Christ Impulse brought men the possibility of once more grasping their personalities, but now of doing so through inner forces. Christ Himself had to unite His cosmic destiny with mankind, so that in the continual fluctuation of the balance between Ahriman and Lucifer men should not fall away from their onward path.

Lucifer turns men's hearts from interest in other men. Luciferic natures take very little interest in their fellows; they grow stiff and hard, considering as right only what they themselves think and feel, and they are not accessible to the opinions of others.

The ahrimanic is particularly revealed by a man not being willing to live among other men as a personality among other personalities but wanting to develop power in the way I referred to yesterday—wanting to rule by exploiting the weaknesses of others."

Ahriman Influence on the Inner Planets

Man's Life on Earth and in the Spiritual Worlds, Rudolf Steiner, Lecture V, London, November 16, 1922, GA 218

"Whilst the luciferic spirits build, as we said, their strongholds in the air, in order to fight for the moral—as against the Earthly—element in man, the ahrimanic beings struggle to harden man; they want to make him like themselves. And their efforts, which have actually been going on for thousands of years, have in fact succeeded in producing a whole race of sub-human beings. They are there, in the elements of Earth and water, a sub-human race. They draw out of a human being his instinctive nature and make of it an Earth-and-water being. These Earth-water beings inhabit the strata immediately below the surface of the Earth. They are beings that have been snatched out of man in the moment of death.

The ahrimanic beings persist in believing they will ultimately be able in this way to entice such a vast number of human beings into their own race and that the Earth will one day be peopled entirely with such ahrimanic sub-human beings. By this means they hope to make the Earth itself immortal, so that the hour may never come for it to perish and be dispersed in cosmic space.

A fearful war is waged all the time between the air-fire beings and the Earth-water beings; they fight to get possession of man. And it is important that man should be aware of this war that is perpetually being waged for him; he must not be blind to it.

Moon, Mercury, Venus, Jupiter, Mars and Saturn live at peace with one another and are held in balance by the Sun; they wage a double fight for the possession of man. First of all, there is the conflict that goes on between the ahrimanic and the luciferic beings; and then we have on the one hand, the fight that is put up by the luciferic beings against the planetary forces beyond the Sun—the Mars, Jupiter, and Saturn influences—whilst on the other hand the ahrimanic forces are waging war on the influences that proceed from Moon, Venus, and Mercury.

Luciferic and ahrimanic beings never relinquish the belief that they will one day achieve their ends, and they are therefore always ready to begin the fight over again. For, time after time, when they think they are on their way to success, they experience frustration and disappointment. This kind of being may indeed be said to live in a mood that oscillates between jubilation and triumph on the one side and constantly recurring disappointment on the other.

For when someone turns liar,—well, that can be ameliorated in the further course of karma; whereas if Lucifer were really to gain the victory he seeks, the Earth would lose that human soul, it would soar right away above the Earth. If, on the other hand, Ahriman were to conquer, or come near to conquering, in the ether body, then the person would become possessed— possessed by his own cleverness.

At the present time, when you cross the threshold, you find yourself only in the midst of the terrific conflict of which we have spoken, between beings of the upper planets who have remained behind in their evolution—immature Mars, Jupiter and Saturn beings—and beings of the lower planets who have remained behind—immature Moon, Mercury and Venus beings. The fight goes on with such fury that the Sun becomes, first of all, fiery and aflame and then grows darker and darker until at last it shows like a terrible black disk. Then we are guided to turn our eyes to the Christ, Christ stands before us, the Spirit Being who, through the Mystery of Golgotha, united Himself with the Earth. And He says to us: Be not dismayed that the Sun has become black; it is black because I, the God of the Sun, am no longer in it; for I have come down and united myself with Earth.

And if, with inner devotion, and with quick and sensitive recognition of all that a knowledge of the Mystery of Golgotha can bring, we draw near to Christ, the Sun begins to make audible for us what Christ is saying to us. When therefore we speak of Christ today, we are speaking of One who can be at our side here on Earth as our Leader, guiding us out of the terrible conflict that the luciferic and ahrimanic powers are waging,—with one another and with the worlds of the upper and lower gods."

Ahriman and Error

Manifestations of Karma, Forces of Nature, Volcanic Eruptions, Earthquakes and Epidemics in Relation to Karma, Rudolf Steiner, Lecture VII, May 1910, GA 266

"Our greed, egotism, ambition, pride, vanity, all qualities connected with this inflation of our Ego, this desire to be in the limelight, all this is the result of luciferic temptations in the astral body. If there were nothing else in life but the egotistical impulses and passions born of Lucifer, we should never be able to free ourselves from them.

When we fall into the power of Lucifer, there immediately intervenes a counteraction by powers antagonistic to the luciferic powers. These exercise an opposing force, whereby the luciferic influence may be actually driven out of us. And it is these forces, opponents of the luciferic powers, which add pain to the process resulting from Lucifer's influence. Thus, if the luciferic powers are evil, we must regard pain as something which is given us by benevolent forces, because through pain we escape from the clutches of these evil powers, and do not succumb to them again. Pain, which is the consciousness of the astral body in a wrong waking state, is also that which prevents us from ever again falling prey to the luciferic powers in that realm where we have already succumbed. Thus, pain becomes our schoolmaster in regard to the temptations of the luciferic powers.

Just as we cannot see the world when we have imperfect eyes, so through luciferic influence we are prevented from seeing the external world as it really is. And because of man's incapacity to see the external world as it really is, the ahrimanic influence has been able to insinuate itself into this inaccurate picture. So, it is the luciferic influence on man which has made Ahriman's approach possible. Subjected to the ahrimanic influence we can fall a prey not only to egotistical passions, urges, greed, vanity, and pride, and so forth, but now egotism can affect the human organism to such an extent as to develop organs through which we can see the external world distorted and inaccurate. Ahriman has insinuated himself into this inaccurate picture, and under his influence we succumb not only to inner temptations, but also to error. We fall into untruth in our judgement of the external world and our assertions concerning it. Thus, Ahriman acts from outside; but we have made it possible for him to reach us.

The ahrimanic and luciferic influences are thus never separated. They always react upon one another, and in a certain sense keep a balance. Lucifer manifests outwards from within, Ahriman acts from without, and our picture of the world is formed between the two. And we oscillate between these two influences which lead us—the one to inner conceit, and the other, to illusions about the external world.

The temptations from both sides must be especially resisted by anyone who is called to a spiritual development, and who wishes to penetrate into the spiritual world, whether by penetrating into that external spirituality which lies behind the phenomena of the external world, or whether by descending mystically into his own inner being. When we penetrate the world which lies behind the physical world, we always find those deceptive images which Ahriman conjures up. When a man tries to descend mystically into his own soul, he is exposed to the temptations of Lucifer in a special degree.

There is but one power before which Lucifer retreats, and that is morality which burns him like the most dreadful of fires. And there is no means by which to oppose Ahriman other than a power of judgement and discernment schooled by Spiritual Science. For Ahriman flees in terror from the wholesome power of judgement acquired upon Earth. In the main there is nothing to which he has a greater aversion than the qualities we gain from a healthy education of our Ego-consciousness. For we shall see that Ahriman belongs to a very different region far removed from that force of sound judgement which we develop in ourselves. The moment Ahriman encounters this, he receives a terrible shock, for this is something completely unknown to him, and he fears it. The more we apply ourselves in our life to develop this wholesome judgement, the more do we work in opposition to Ahriman. In fact, the best remedy against the particularly harmful diseases which result in visions and delusory voices induced by Ahriman is to make all efforts to induce the person to acquire a wholesome and rational judgement.

Lucifer has an aversion for humility and modesty in man and is repulsed if we have only such an opinion of ourselves as a wholesome judgement entitles us to hold. He is present whenever the qualities of vanity and ambition arise. All this and the illusions which we engender about ourselves, prepare us to receive Ahriman as well. Nothing can defend us against Ahriman unless we really make an effort to think wholesomely, as life between birth and death teaches us to do. Certainly—but there is only one healthy path by which we can enter, and that is the morality that must be acquired upon Earth, a morality in the highest sense of the word, which will keep us from over-estimation of ourselves, and will make us less subservient to our impulses, greed and passions, but which on the other hand will be an active, wholesome co-operation with the conditions of Earth life, and not a desire to soar above such conditions.

Whatever is to be traced to ahrimanic influence is indirectly attributable to Lucifer; when, however, the luciferic influence has been so strong as immediately to call forth the ahrimanic influence, then this influence is the more malicious. It anchors itself not only in the transgressions of the astral body, but in those of the etheric body. It manifests itself in a consciousness lying deeper than our pain consciousness, causing damage not necessarily accompanied by pain, damage that renders useless the organ which it attacks.

A counteracting effect comes into play, however, just as we have the effect of pain counteracting the luciferic influence. This counteracting effect will operate in such a way that the moment there is any danger of our being linked too closely with the physical world of the senses, and of our losing the forces which lead us up into the spiritual world, in that moment the organ is destroyed; it will either be paralyzed or else rendered too weak to be effective. A process of destruction takes place. Thus, if we see an organ approaching destruction, we must realize that we owe this to beneficial forces; the organ is taken from us so that we may find our way back into the spiritual world. When there is no alternative of escape, certain forces do in fact destroy our organs or weaken them so that we may not become too greatly entangled in Maya or illusion and may find our way back into the spiritual world.

The good we have attained through Lucifer is the possibility of discrimination between good and evil, the free faculty of discrimination, and our free will. All this we may attain only through Lucifer. Our greed, egotism, ambition, pride, vanity, all qualities connected with this inflation of our Ego, this desire to be in the limelight, all this is the result of luciferic temptations in the astral body. If there were nothing else in life but the egotistical impulses and passions born of Lucifer, we should never be able to free ourselves from them.

When we fall into the power of Lucifer, there immediately intervenes a counteraction by powers antagonistic to the luciferic powers. These exercise an opposing force, whereby the luciferic influence may be actually driven out of us. And it is these forces, opponents of the luciferic powers, which add pain to the process resulting from Lucifer's influence. Thus, if the luciferic powers are evil, we must regard pain as something which is given us by benevolent forces, because through pain we escape from the clutches of these evil powers, and do not succumb to them again. Pain, which is the consciousness of the astral body in a wrong waking state, is also that which prevents us from ever again falling prey to the luciferic powers in that realm where we have already succumbed. Thus, pain becomes our schoolmaster in regard to the temptations of the luciferic powers.

Just as we cannot see the world when we have imperfect eyes, so through luciferic influence we are prevented from seeing the external world as it really is. And because of man's incapacity to see the external world as it really is, the ahrimanic influence has been able to insinuate itself into this inaccurate picture. So, it is the luciferic influence on man which has made Ahriman's approach possible. Subjected to the ahrimanic influence we can fall a prey not only to egotistical passions, urges, greed, vanity, and pride, and so forth, but now egotism can affect the human organism to such an extent as to develop organs through which we can see the external world distorted and inaccurate. Ahriman has insinuated himself into this inaccurate picture, and under his influence we succumb not only to inner temptations, but also to error. We fall into untruth in our judgement of the external world and our assertions concerning it. Thus, Ahriman acts from outside; but we have made it possible for him to reach us.

The ahrimanic and luciferic influences are thus never separated. They always react upon one another, and in a certain sense keep a balance. Lucifer manifests outwards from within, Ahriman acts from without, and our picture of the world is formed between the two. And we oscillate between these two influences which lead us—the one to inner conceit, and the other to illusions about the external world.

The temptations from both sides must be especially resisted by anyone who is called to a spiritual development, and who wishes to penetrate into the spiritual world, whether by penetrating into that external spirituality which lies behind the phenomena of the external world, or whether by descending mystically into his own inner being. When we penetrate the world which lies behind the physical world, we always find those deceptive images which Ahriman conjures up. When a man tries to descend mystically into his own soul, he is exposed to the temptations of Lucifer in a special degree.

There is but one power before which Lucifer retreats, and that is morality which burns him like the most dreadful of fires. And there is no means by which to oppose Ahriman other than a power of judgement and discernment schooled by Spiritual Science. For Ahriman flees in terror from the wholesome power of judgement acquired upon Earth. In the main there is nothing to which he has a greater aversion than the qualities we gain from a healthy education of our Ego-consciousness. For we shall see that Ahriman belongs to a very different region far removed from that force of sound judgement which we develop in ourselves. The moment Ahriman encounters this, he receives a terrible shock, for this is something completely unknown to him, and he fears it. The more we apply ourselves in our life to develop this wholesome judgement, the more do we work in opposition to Ahriman. In fact, the best remedy against the particularly harmful diseases which result in visions and delusory voices induced by Ahriman is to make all efforts to induce the person to acquire a wholesome and rational judgement.

Lucifer has an aversion for humility and modesty in man and is repulsed if we have only such an opinion of ourselves as a wholesome judgement entitles us to hold. He is present whenever the qualities of vanity and ambition arise. All this and the illusions which we engender about ourselves, prepare us to receive Ahriman as well. Nothing can defend us against Ahriman unless we really make an effort to think wholesomely, as life between birth and death teaches us to do. Certainly there is only one healthy path by which we can enter, and that is the morality that must be acquired upon Earth, a morality in the highest sense of the word, which will keep us from over-estimation of ourselves, and will make us less subservient to our impulses, greed and passions, but which on the other hand will be an active, wholesome co-operation with the conditions of Earth life, and not a desire to soar above such conditions.

Whatever is to be traced to ahrimanic influence is indirectly attributable to Lucifer; when, however, the luciferic influence has been so strong as immediately to call forth the ahrimanic influence, then this influence is the more malicious. It anchors itself not only in the transgressions of the astral body, but in those of the etheric body. It manifests itself in a consciousness lying deeper than our pain consciousness, causing damage not necessarily accompanied by pain, damage that renders useless the organ which it attacks.

A counteracting effect comes into play, however, just as we have the effect of pain counteracting the luciferic influence. This counteracting effect will operate in such a way that the moment there is any danger of our being linked too closely with the physical world of the senses, and of our losing the forces which lead us up into the spiritual world, in that moment the organ is destroyed; it will either be paralyzed or else rendered too weak to be effective. A process of destruction takes place. Thus, if we see an organ approaching destruction, we must realize that we owe this to beneficial forces; the organ is taken from us so that we may find our way back into the spiritual world. When there is no alternative of escape, certain forces do in fact destroy our organs or weaken them so that we may not become too greatly entangled in Maya or illusion and may find our way back into the spiritual world.

The good we have attained through Lucifer is the possibility of discrimination between good and evil, the free faculty of discrimination, and our free will. All this we may attain only through Lucifer."

Balancing Ahriman and Lucifer

The Balance in the World and Man, Lucifer and Ahriman, The World as Product of the Working of Balance, Rudolf Steiner, Dornach, November 20, 1914, GA 158

"Experiences deriving from the influences of Lucifer and Ahriman are all the time playing into human life. In this basic experience of man during the Fourth Post-Atlantean or Greco-Roman epoch, Lucifer's influence was the greater; in our own epoch, Ahriman is the predominant influence. Lucifer is connected with all those experiences which, lacking the definition imparted by the senses, remain undifferentiated and obscure.

Everything that is associated with questioning and doubt, with feelings of dissatisfaction caused when something in the world demands an answer and we are thrown back entirely upon our own resources—all this is connected with the luciferic powers. An over-exuberant, too widely extended ether-body gives rise to an excessively vigorous breathing process, and this provides the luciferic forces with opportunity to work. The luciferic forces, then, can make their way into the human being when the ether-body has expanded beyond the normal. The luciferic forces also operate in the blood, permeating and surging through it.

The ether-body is too small now, and this will become more marked as evolution proceeds. If it can be said that in the man of ancient Greece, the ether-body was too large, it can be said that in the man of modern times the ether-body is compressed and contracted, has become too small. The more human beings are led by materialism to disdain the Spiritual, the more will the ether-body contract and wither. The physical body too will always tend to dry up, to wither, if the contraction of the ether-body is excessive. Now into this dried-up ether-body, Ahriman can insinuate himself, just as Lucifer can creep into an extended, diffuse ether-body. Ahriman will assume the form which indicates a lack of power in the ether-body.

Just as those etheric forces which tend towards the luciferic nature can only find easy access to the blood by way of the breath, so the etheric forces which tend towards the ahrimanic nature can only approach the nervous system. Ahriman is deprived of the possibility of penetrating into the blood because he cannot come near the warmth of the blood.

Just as the Greek confronted the Sphinx whose field of operation is the breathing system, so the man of the Fifth Post-Atlantean Epoch confronts Mephistopheles who operates in the nerve-process, who is cold and scornful because he is bloodless, because he lacks the warmth that belongs to the blood. He is the scoffer, the cold, scornful companion of man.

Just as it was the task of Oedipus to get the better of the Sphinx, so it is the task of man in the Fifth Post-Atlantean Epoch to get the better of Mephistopheles. The human being of the modern age is confronted by the fruits of intellect and cold reason, rooted as they are in the nerve-process.

Whereas the child in Greece was tormented by a flood of questions, the suffering awaiting the human being of our modern time is rather that of being in the grip of preconceptions and prejudices, of having as an incubus at his side a second "body" consisting of all these preconceived judgments and opinions.

The Mephistophelean nature is strengthened by all the prejudices and limitations of materialism, and a future can already be perceived when everyone will be born with a second being by his side, a being who whispers to him of the foolishness of those who speak of the reality of the spiritual world. Accompanied by this second being, he will feel the urge to think materialistic thoughts, to think, not through his own being, but through the second being who is his companion.

In an ether-body that has been parched by materialism, Mephistopheles will be able to dwell. The ether-body must be quickened in order that the human being may be able to take his rightful stand, fully cognizant of the nature of the being who stands at his side. If he does not understand the nature of this second being, he will be spellbound by him, fettered to him.

If adults whose task it is to educate children today do not know how to deal rightly with what comes to expression in the child, human nature itself will be impaired owing to a lack of understanding of the wiles of Mephistopheles.

When Ahriman is beside us, we are perpetually in danger of falling victim to him, of giving ourselves over to him to such an extent that we cannot get free. In face of the Sphinx, the human being is aware of something that penetrates him and as it were tears him to pieces. In face of the Mephistophelean influence, he feels that he must yield to it, bind himself to it, and succumb to it.

But just as it was the task of the Greek, through the development of conscious ego-hood, to conquer the Sphinx, so we, in our age, must get the better of Mephistopheles by enriching the Ego with the wisdom that can be born only from knowledge and investigation of the spiritual world, from Spiritual Science.

In their rightfully allotted place, Lucifer and Ahriman work beneficially; in their wrongful place—there they are injurious. The nerve-process—which works, not from without but from within the Ego, must here be strengthened. Thus is the ahrimanic power taken into the human being and put in its right place.

The man of the Fifth Post-Atlantean Epoch, who confronts Ahriman-Mephistopheles, must take Lucifer into himself. Everything that the Ego accumulates in the head must be pressed down into the rest of man's nature.

The Ahriman-nature in Oedipus has to get the better of Lucifer; the Lucifer-nature in Faust has to help him to overcome Ahriman-Mephistopheles. Ahriman-Mephistopheles operates more in the external world, Lucifer more in the inner life.

In the man of the modern age, the Ego has become too strong, and he must break free. But this he can only do by deepening his knowledge of spiritual happenings, of the world to which the Ego truly belongs. The Ego must know that it is a citizen of the spiritual world, not merely the inhabitant of a human body. This is the demand of the age in which we ourselves are living. The man of the Fourth Post-Atlantean Epoch was called upon to strive with might and main for consciousness in the physical body; the man of the Fifth Post-Atlantean Epoch must strive to become conscious in the spiritual world, so to expand his consciousness that it reaches into the spiritual world."

Ahriman and Lucifer Work Together

Secrets of the Threshold, Rudolf Steiner, Lecture VIII, August 31, 1913, GA 147

"Lucifer and Ahriman now are in league together in a kind of partnership in the outer world. Before these forces reach the human soul, they are knotted together externally. In ancient times the skeins of influence from Ahriman and Lucifer were quite separate, but nowadays we have them tangled and knotted together within the development of our civilization. It is extremely difficult for a human being to unravel the entanglement and find a way out of it. We need to be watchful of the chaotic entanglement of luciferic and ahrimanic threads. For no one today is more challenged to come to terms with these forces than he who is on the path of spiritual knowledge.

On the threshold, the luciferic impulses assert themselves strongly from within, and when the human soul tends to deaden its awareness, Lucifer immediately unites with Ahriman, with the result that the entrance to the spiritual world is barred.

At the very moment when we get rid of the results of our egoism, Lucifer and Ahriman have an easy game with the soul: in partnership, it is not at all difficult for them to lead the human soul into their special kingdom where they can produce all sorts of spiritual worlds, which the human being will take for the truly genuine one grounded in the cosmic order."

Ahriman in Meditation

Esoteric Lessons, Rudolf Steiner, Part III, Stockholm, June 8, 1913, GA 266

"In a theosophical lecture everyone is called upon to be active; in a lecture with slides Ahriman is summoned to think for the people. Materialists are the greatest conjurers of spirits. Every materialistic gathering is nothing else than a conjuring of Ahriman, because basically people are afraid of the spirit in their soul.

Esoteric pupils often come and complain about thoughts that attack them during meditation. It's really a sign of progress that one senses these thoughts; it shows that we don't just have Lucifer and Ahriman in us anymore, but that we begin to see them outside us as powers, for thoughts that arise like this are entirely from Lucifer and Ahriman. If everything had remained as originally intended, then after the luciferic temptation a man wouldn't have been able to forget his thoughts. He would always have had access to the Akashic records, but it would have been Lucifer and Ahriman who wrote up this chronicle for him. That's why the good Gods had to arrange things so that a man can also forget his thoughts. Everything that sinks into the unconscious like this is dead and Lucifer and Ahriman eat it up. They make it a part of their being and it comes out again in men's meditation as luciferic and ahrimanic things.

As soon as someone starts to meditate the hope arises in Lucifer: Maybe I'll be victorious in the world yet. And then he attacks the man with his discarded thoughts. A man really loves to go from one thought to another, and he doesn't love to remain filled with one thought-content in reflection. A man doesn't really love the spirit at all. He must force himself to keep certain thoughts in his soul for an extended period. A man really loves Lucifer and Ahriman."

Ahriman and Falsehood

Morality and Karma, Rudolf Steiner, Nuremberg, November 12, 1910, GA 135

"We know that the human soul passes through many incarnations and that there was a moment in the development of mankind when the tempters, Lucifer and Ahriman, crept into the human soul. Ahriman lives in the etheric body and Lucifer in the astral body of man.

Lucifer is a power that tempts the human soul by drawing it down morally and by leading it away from its origin. He casts us into the depths of Earthly nature, and we should beware of this. Lucifer is the power that draws us down into the depths of passion.

Ahriman, on the other hand, is the spirit of falsehood and error and he falsifies our judgments. Both Lucifer and Ahriman are powers which are hostile to human progress. Yet they get on very well with each other. Envy is a quality in which the luciferic power comes to expression. When a person first discovers that his soul is filled with envy, he begins to fight against Lucifer, the source of envy. What does Lucifer do in that case? He simply hands over the matter to Ahriman, and Ahriman darkens the human judgment.

When we fight against Lucifer in the astral body, Ahriman can easily insinuate himself into the etheric body, darkening our judgments on other people. This is falsehood and falsehood is an ahrimanic quality.

People also feel a strong dislike for falsehood, and they try to fight against it. When we try to overcome falsehood, we can see that Ahriman hands over the sceptre to Lucifer, so that a quality creeps into the astral body which appears in the form of an extremely pronounced Egoism. Egoism is restrained falsehood. These two qualities, falsehood and envy, are a crass expression of the way in which Lucifer and Ahriman work within the human soul."

Ahriman and Lucifer in Art

Old and New Methods of Initiation, Rudolf Steiner, Lecture I, Dornach, January 1, 1922, GA 210

"In ordinary consciousness, we are on the whole unaware of the two dangers which can cause us to deviate from our state of balance towards one side or the other, towards the luciferic or the ahrimanic side.

When we are small, perhaps tiny, children, the youthful, luciferic forces predominate. But even then, deep down, are the ageing forces, the forces which eventually lead to the sclerosis of our body and, in the end, to death. It is necessary for both kinds of force to exist in the human body. Through the luciferic forces there is always a possibility of inclining towards, let me say, the phosphoric side, towards warmth. In the extreme situation of an illness, this manifests in a fever such as a pleuritic condition, a state of inflammation. This inclination towards fever and inflammation is ever-present and is only held in check or in balance by those other forces which want to lead towards solidified, sclerotic, mineral states. The nature of the human being arises from the state of balance between these two polar-opposite forces.

Organs, such as heart, lungs, liver, are seen to encompass polar opposites which incline them on the one hand towards dissolution into warmth and, on the other hand, towards consolidation into the mineral state. For instance, that at the change of teeth, around the seventh year, ahrimanic forces are setting to work in the head region; or that when the physical body starts to develop towards the warmth pole at puberty, this means that luciferic forces are at work; that in the rhythmical nature of the human being there are constant swings of the pendulum, physically too, between the luciferic and the ahrimanic aspect.

Turning now to the soul element, in a higher sense the second element of man's being, we find the ahrimanic influence at work in everything that drives the soul towards purely intellectual rigid laws. Our natural science today is almost totally ahrimanic. As we develop towards ahrimanic soul elements, we discard anything that might fill our concepts and ideas with warmth. We submit only to whatever makes concepts and ideas ice-cold and dry as dust. Also, when we imbue our soul with moral issues, the ahrimanic influence is found in everything that tends towards what is pedantic, stiff, philistine on the one hand; but also, in what tends towards freedom, towards independence, towards everything that strives to extract the fruits of material existence from this material existence and wants to become perfect by filling material existence.

The luciferic influence in the human soul is found in everything that makes us desire to fly upwards out of ourselves. This can create nebulous, mystical attitudes which lead us to regions where any thought of the material world seems ignoble and inferior. Thus, we are led astray, misled into despising material existence entirely and into wanting instead to indulge in whatever lies above the material world, into wanting wings on which to soar above Earthly existence, at least in our soul. This is how the luciferic aspect works on our soul. To the ahrimanic aspect of dull, dry, cold science is added a sultry mysticism of the kind that in religions leads to an ascetic disdain for the Earth, and so on.

Luciferic forces endow human beings with the possibility of expressing the spirit in the semblance of sense-perceptible existence. It is for this that all art and all beauty are striving. Lucifer is the guardian of beauty and art. So, in seeking the right balance between luciferic and ahrimanic influences we may allow art—Lucifer—in the form of beauty, to work upon this balance. There is no question of saying that human beings must guard against ahrimanic and luciferic influences. What matters is for human beings to find the right attitude towards ahrimanic and luciferic influences, while always maintaining a balance between the two. Lucifer strives to lead human beings away from the reality in which they find themselves between birth and death into a reality which was indeed reality in earlier times, but which cannot be genuine reality for the present day.

During the period from Augustine to Galileo, human beings had to resist the luciferic element in their striving for balance. And in more recent times human beings have to resist the ahrimanic element in their striving for balance."

Ahriman in Art

Secrets of the Threshold, Rudolf Steiner, Lecture VI, August 29, 1913, GA 147

"We tried to show through the teachings of Benedictus (in the Mystery Dramas) how the luciferic, the ahrimanic and the middle condition work into the triad of thought, word and writing in the development of human culture.

Of the five arts, architecture and sculpture are those most particularly open to the ahrimanic impulse. To accomplish anything in architecture and sculpture we must find our way into the form element, which is dominant on the physical plane, for here the Spirits of Form are the ruling forces. To get to know them, one must plunge into their spiritual element, as I said before, when speaking figuratively of putting one's head into an ant hill. A person who has anything to do with sculpture must plunge his head into the living element of the Spirits of Form. In the realm of the physical world these Spirits work cooperatively with the ahrimanic element.

We should always realize that such beings as the luciferic and ahrimanic ones have their particular domains, where normally they live and work, and that bad effects come about only when they overstep their boundaries. The ahrimanic impulses have their absolutely legitimate domain in architecture and sculpture.

On the other hand, we find that music and poetry are two arts where luciferic impulses are at work. Just as thought takes place in the solitude of the soul and thereby separates it from the rest of the world, the experience of music and poetry, too, belongs to our inner nature where these arts directly meet the luciferic impulse.

In architecture it is generally the case that the ahrimanic impulse is the stronger, but in sculpture the luciferic influence opposing Ahriman can be so strong that in some sculptural works Lucifer is more dominant than Ahriman. There can be luciferic sculpture and though poetry is chiefly under the influence of Lucifer, the ahrimanic influence can work very strongly on music, so that we can find music with more of Ahriman than of Lucifer.

In the realm of painting, we are in the highest degree vulnerable to one or the other influence. The middle line is always the place where we have to bring about, in the very strictest sense of the word, the harmonious balance of polarities by means of human will and human action."

Ahriman and Mystery Wisdom

Occult Science—An Outline, Rudolf Steiner, Chapter IV, *Man and the Evolution of the World*, GA 013

"The more man turned his interest to the physical world, the greater was the possibility for Ahriman to find his way into the soul during Earthly life, and then maintain his power over it after death. In Earthly life the power of Ahriman misleads man into regarding the sense-perceptible, physical existence as the one and only reality, thus shutting himself off entirely from any kind of outlook into a spiritual world. In the spiritual world, Ahriman brings man to complete isolation, leading him to center all his interest upon himself alone. Humans who at death are in the power of Ahriman are born again as egoists.

After the intervention of Ahriman another kind of initiation was added. Ahriman had, since the middle of the Atlantean epoch, veiled all that of the spiritual world which would, but for his intervention, have appeared behind the perceptions of the physical senses. This was now unveiled to the initiates. It was revealed to them that spiritual powers underlay the forces of nature. They could tell of spiritual beings behind outer nature. It was given them to behold the divine creative powers underlying the forces that are at work in the realms of Nature beneath man. All that had worked on from Old Saturn, Old Sun, and Old Moon, forming man's physical body, life-body and astral body, as well as the mineral, plant and animal kingdoms of nature—all this made up the content of one kind of mystery-secrets. These were the secrets over which Ahriman held his hand. What had led, on the other hand, to the sentient soul, intellectual soul and spiritual soul, was made manifest in a second kind of mystery-secrets. But there was something of which the mysteries could only tell prophetically, namely that in the fullness of time a human being would appear with an astral body such that, in spite of Lucifer, the light-world of the spirit and the Sun would come to consciousness in him through the life-body, apart from any special states of soul. And the physical body of this human being would be such that for him the realms of the spiritual world which Ahriman is able to conceal until physical death occurs would become manifest."

Physical Description of Ahriman

Karmic Relationships, Ahriman's Fight Against the Michael Principle, The Message of Michael, Rudolf Steiner, Volume III, Lecture VIII, GA 237

"The very strongest efforts are being made by Ahriman to acquire the Intelligence that has come into the hands of men. For if men once became possessed by Ahriman, Ahriman himself, in human heads, would be possessing the Intelligence. In Ahriman there stands before us a cosmic Being of the highest imaginable Intelligence, a cosmic Being who has already taken the Intelligence entirely into the individual, personal element.

To reproduce Ahriman in human imaginations we should have to give him a receding forehead, a frivolously cynical expression, for in him everything comes out of the lower forces, and yet from these lower forces the highest intelligence proceeds. If ever we let ourselves in for a discussion with Ahriman, we should inevitably be shattered by the logical conclusiveness, the magnificent certainty of aim with which he manipulates his arguments. Every ahrimanic being is over-endowed with personal intelligence in the way I have now described; critical to a degree in the repudiation of all things illogical; scornful and contemptuous in thought."

Ahrimanic Possession

Karmic Relationships, The Working of Ahriman into the Once Cosmic and Now Personal Intelligence, Rudolf Steiner, Volume III, Lecture X, GA 237

"We must understand that since Michael no longer draws out the soul-and-spirit from the physical bodily nature as in times past, Ahriman can play his game with the soul-and-spirit as it lives within the body. Above all when the soul-spiritual is highly gifted and is yet firmly fastened in the body, then especially it can be exposed to Ahriman. Precisely in the most gifted of men does Ahriman find his prey,—so as to tear the Intelligence from Michael, remove it far from Michael.

The ahrimanic spirits, though they cannot incarnate, can incorporate themselves; temporarily they can penetrate human souls, permeate human bodies. In such moments the brilliant and overpowering spirit of an ahrimanic Intelligence is stronger than anything that the individual being possesses,—far, far stronger. Then, however intelligent he may be, however much he may have learned, and especially if his physical body is thoroughly taken hold of by all his learning, an ahrimanic spirit can for a time incorporate itself in him. Then it is Ahriman who looks out of his eyes, Ahriman who moves his fingers, Ahriman who blows his nose, Ahriman who walks.

Ahriman is a great and outstanding Intelligence, and Ahriman's purpose with Earthly evolution is overwhelming and thorough. He makes use of every opportunity. If the Spiritual has implanted itself so strongly in the bodily nature of a human being,—if the bodily nature is taken hold of by the Spirit to such an extent that the consciousness is thereby in a measure stunned or lowered or impaired,—Ahriman uses this opportunity. And then it happens (for in our age this has become possible) then it happens that a brilliant spirit takes possession of the human being, overpowering the human personality; and such a spirit, dwelling within a human personality and overpowering him, is able to work upon Earth—able to work just like a human being.

I have told you, my dear friends, of what will be fulfilled at the end of this century, with those who now come to the things of the Spirit and take them in full earnestness and sincerity. This is the time above all, which the ahrimanic spirits wish to use most strongly. This is the time they want to use, because human beings are so completely wrapped up in the Intelligence that has come over them. They have become so unbelievably clever. But of a truth, the cleverness which is thus cultivated is used by Ahriman. And when moreover the bodies are especially adapted to a possible lowering or diminution of consciousness, it may happen that Ahriman himself emerges, incorporated in human form. Twice already it can be demonstrated that Ahriman has thus appeared as an author. For Ahriman by his brilliant gifts can find his way into everything—he can slip into the very style of a man. He has a way of approach to all things."

Christ as Antidote to Ahriman

The Michael Mystery, Michael's Task in the Sphere of Ahriman,
Rudolf Steiner, Chapter IV, GA 26

"What was thus accomplished five hundred years ago for Man's consciousness, had already taken place on a broader scale throughout his general being at the time when the Mystery of Golgotha entered upon its Earthly manifestation. This was the time when human evolution began— imperceptibly as yet for the consciousness of most people of that period— to slide gradually down, out of a world where Ahriman has but little power, into one where he has very much. It was in the fifteenth century that this downslide, from one world-stratum into another, reached its final completion.

Here, in this world-stratum, it becomes possible for Ahriman to exert his influence upon Man, and with disastrous effects, because in this stratum the divine influences congenial to Man have died out. But there was no other possible way for Man to arrive at the development of his free will, save by withdrawing to a sphere in which those Divine Spirit-beings had no life, who were involved with him from his origin.

But these Divine Beings have sent Christ from the Sun to Earth. He, for the salvation of mankind, has united His own living Being with the deadness of divine existence in the kingdom of Ahriman. Mankind has thus the twofold possibility, which is the pledge of their freedom: Either to turn to Christ in that mind and spirit which was theirs subconsciously when they came down from the vision of super-sensible life in the Spirit until they could use Intelligence,—but to do this now in consciousness. Or else, in their detachment from Spirit-life, to seek to enjoy the sense of themselves—and thereby fall a prey to the Powers of Ahriman and be carried in the ahrimanic direction of evolution.

Whatever Michael performs, is performed in such a way as to exert no influence from his part upon man; but they are free to follow him, and so, in freedom, with the Christ-Power to find their way out again from Ahriman's sphere, which they entered of necessity."

Michaelic and Ahrimanic Thinking

The Michael Mystery, World-Thoughts in Michael and World-Thoughts in Ahriman, Rudolf Steiner, Chapter IX, GA 026

"Ahriman acquired possession of the intellectual force at a time when he could not convert it into inward life. It remained in his being as a force that has nothing to do with the heart and soul. A chill and frosty, soulless cosmic impulse is the intellectual power as it streams from Ahriman.

Archangel Michael has never appropriated the power of intellect to himself. He administers it as a divine spiritual force, feeling himself in union with the divine spiritual powers. And this intellectual force, when Michael wields it, shews itself to be as well capable of being made an expression of the heart and soul, as of the head and mind. Michael reigns through the course of Time, bearing the light of the Cosmos as living being of his being, fashioning the warmth of the Cosmos as revelation of his own being. He wends as one Being like a World—affirming himself inasmuch only as he affirms the World—as though from all stations of the universe guiding forces to the Earth below.

Ahriman, in his course, from time would wring Space. Around him is darkness, into which he projects the rays of his own light. The more he achieves his ends, the keener grows the frost about him. He moves like a world contracted into one single being—his own; affirming himself only by negating the world; he moves, as though he brought with him uncanny forces from the dark caverns of the Earth.

When Man, in the enjoyment of his freedom, lets himself be seduced by Ahriman, he becomes caught up into the intellectual process as into a spiritual automatism, in which he is a bit of the machinery, no longer himself."

Defeating Ahriman with Sound Judgment

Manifestations of Karma, Karma of the Higher Beings, Rudolf Steiner, Lecture VIII, May 25, 1910, GA 120

"Whilst acting upon us, the luciferic influences call forth the ahrimanic influences whose forces do not act from within, but from without, working upon and in us by means of all that confronts us externally. Thus, it is Ahriman who is evoked by Lucifer, and we human beings are vitally involved in the conflict of these two principles. When we find ourselves caught in the clutches of either Lucifer or Ahriman, we must endeavour to progress by triumphing over the ill that has been inflicted upon us.

This interplay of activity of the luciferic and ahrimanic powers around us can be understood quite clearly if we consider the case where the person succumbs to ahrimanic influence, whereby he experiences all kinds of deceptive images and illusions. He believes that knowledge of one thing or another has been specially imparted to him or is in one direction or another making an impression upon him, while another person who had preserved a sound power of judgement would easily recognize that the person in question has succumbed to errors and delusions. There is no other or at least no more favourable defence against the delusions of false clairvoyants than a sound power of judgement acquired during our physical life between birth and death."

Christ Between Lucifer and Ahriman

The Cosmic New Year, The Michael Path to Christ,
Rudolf Steiner, December 25, 1919, Lecture II, GA 195

"The more we seek to get rid of Lucifer, the more we are dominated by him, for it was necessary during thousands of years of human evolution to enter into the inheritance of the incarnated Lucifer. Then came the Mystery of Golgotha. And a time will come in the future when, just as Lucifer was incorporated in the East in an Earthly personality, to prepare for Christianity among the heathen, so in the West there will take place an Earthly incarnation of Ahriman himself. This time is approaching. Ahriman will appear, objectively, on the Earth. Just as truly as Lucifer has walked the Earth, and as Christ has walked the Earth, objectively, in human form, so will Ahriman walk the Earth, bringing with him an extraordinary increase of power to Earthly human understanding. We men have not the task of hindering in any way this incarnation of Ahriman, but it is our task so to prepare humanity beforehand, that Ahriman may be estimated in the right way. For Ahriman will have tasks, he will have to do this and that, and men must value rightly and make a right use of that which, through Ahriman, comes into the world. Men will only be able to do this if they are able to adjust themselves now in the right way to that which Ahriman is already sending to the Earth from the worlds beyond in order that he may control the economic life upon Earth without being noticed. This must not be. Ahriman must not control the Economic life on the Earth without his being noticed. We must thoroughly learn to know his particular qualities. We must be able to oppose him with full consciousness.

It is most important for man at the present time to place Christ in the center between Ahriman and Lucifer. The Christ power must permeate us. But as men we must always seek the balance between the mystic enthusiasm which tends to lift us above ourselves, and the materialistic understanding which by its bourgeois heaviness drags us down to Earth. At every moment we must seek the balance between the luciferic impulses which lift us up, and the ahrimanic which drag us down. In the effort to gain this balance we find the Christ.

It is the great error of modern times that world-evolution should be represented as a duality, whereas it should be represented as a trinity. One set of forces are the upward-striving luciferic forces which approach man in mysticism, in sentimentalism, in fantasy—in what in fantasy is degenerate, fantastic; these forces dwell in man's blood. The second are the ahrimanic forces which dwell in all that is dry, heavy, in the bony system. The Christ stands in the middle between these two. His is the third group of forces. Lucifer's is the first, Ahriman's the second, and in the center between the two, is the Christ-force."

Christ Uses Ahriman

Exoteric and Esoteric Christianity, Rudolf Steiner, Dornach, April 2, 1922, GA 211

"Thus, the Mystery of Golgotha meant this for the gods: a greater wealth of knowledge through the wisdom of death. If a god had not passed through death, the whole Earth would have become entirely intellectual, without ever reaching the evolution which the gods had planned for it from the very beginning.

Now the Christ taught his initiates that he came from a world where death was unknown; he learnt to know death, here on Earth, and conquered death. If one understands this connection between the Earthly world and the divine world, it will be possible to lead the intellect back again into spirituality. One must realize that he who understands the entire evolution of mankind knows that the gods have overcome Ahriman by using his forces for the benefit of the Earth, but his power has been broken because the gods themselves learnt to know death in the being of Christ. Indeed, the gods have placed Ahriman into the evolution of the Earth, but in making use of him they have forced him to come down into the evolution of the Earth without completing his own rulership.

He who learns to know Ahriman since the Mystery of Golgotha and he who knew him before, knows that Ahriman has waited for the world-historic moment in which he will not only invade the unconscious and subconscious in man, as in the case since the days of Atlantis but will invade also man's consciousness. Ahriman has waited with longing for the moment in which to invade human consciousness with his power. His purpose was thwarted because he knew nothing of the divine plan whereby a being—the Christ—was to be sent to the Earth, a being who underwent death. Thus, the intervention of Ahriman was possible, but the sharp edge was taken off his rule. Since then, Ahriman uses every opportunity to encourage men in the exclusive use of the intellect.

Special joy lives in Ahriman's soul since the period stretching from the forties of the 19th century until about the end of the 19th century; in the predominant sway of materialism Ahriman could cherish new hopes for his rule over the Earth. In this time even theology becomes materialistic.

If Anthroposophy can again make clear to men the independence of the spirit-soul being which is not dependent on the bodily being, Ahriman will have to give up his hopes for the time. The battle of the Christ against Ahriman is again possible.

Ahriman has, as it were, been forced to enter the evolution of the Earth. Without him, the gods could not have placed intellectualism into mankind and if they had not succeeded in taking off the sharp edge to Ahriman's rule through the Christ event, Ahriman would have rendered the whole Earth intellectual from within and material from without."

Ahriman's Battle with Michael 1840-1879

Fall of the Spirits of Darkness, The Battle between Michael and 'The Dragon', Rudolf Steiner, Lecture IX, Dornach, October 14, 1917, GA 177

"Visualize a battle which continued for decades in the spiritual worlds, from the 1840s until the autumn of 1879. This may be called a battle which the spirits who are followers of the spirit belonging to the hierarchy of Archangels whom we may call Michael fought with certain ahrimanic powers. Please consider this battle to have been in the first place a battle in the spiritual world. Everything I am referring to, at the moment, relates to this battle fought by Michael and his followers against certain ahrimanic powers. The battle thus took place in the 40s, 50s, 60s and 70s and came to a conclusion in the autumn of 1879, when Michael and his followers won a victory over certain ahrimanic powers.

We may say that a particular crowd of ahrimanic spirits seek, over and over again, to bring something into world evolution, but they are always overcome. And so, they also lost the battle in the autumn of 1879.

The late 1870s were a particular time when human souls became subject to ahrimanic powers, with regard to certain powers of perception. Before this, these powers were active in the spiritual realms and therefore left human beings more in peace; when they were driven out of the spiritual realms they came upon human beings. And if we enquire into the nature of the ahrimanic powers which entered into human beings when they had to leave the realms of the spirit, the answer is, the ahrimanic materialistic view with its personal bias. We are thus able to say that due to the presence of these ahrimanic powers from 1879 onwards, personal ambitions and inclinations to interpret the world in materialistic terms came to exist in the human realm.

After one of these battles, for example, the crowd of ahrimanic spirits populated the Earth with the Earthly life-forms which the medical profession now calls bacilli. Everything which has the power to act as a bacillus, everything in which bacilli are involved, is the result of crowds of ahrimanic spirits being cast down from Heaven to Earth at a time when the dragon had been overcome. In the same way the ahrimanic, Mephistophelean way of thinking has spread since the late 1870s as the result of such a victory. Thus we are able to say, that tubercular and bacillary diseases come from a similar source as the materialism which has taken hold of human minds.

Some individuals develop an irresistible hankering for intellectual materialism which arises from being in league with the fallen Ahriman. They gradually come to love the impulses which Ahriman raises in their souls and, indeed, consider them to be a particularly noble and sublime way of thinking. It is because the ahrimanic powers entered into us when Michael won his victory that we are gaining in human freedom. Everything is connected with this, for the crowd of ahrimanic spirits has entered into all of us. We gain in human freedom, but we must be aware of this. We should not allow the ahrimanic powers to gain the upper hand, as it were, and we should not fall in love with them.

This is tremendously important. There always is the danger of people continuing in materialism, in the materialistic, ahrimanic way of thinking, and carrying this on into ages when, according to the plan of things, it should have been overcome. The people who do not turn away from the ahrimanic, materialistic way of thinking and want to keep it, would then be in league with everything which has come about through similar victories won over the dragon by Michael. They therefore would not unite with spiritual progress in human evolution but with material progress. And a time would come in the sixth post-Atlantean age when the only thing to please them would be to live in something which will have been brought about by bacilli, those microscopically small enemies of humanity.

Exactly because of its logical consistency, and indeed its greatness, the scientific way of thinking, too, is in great danger of sliding into the ahrimanic way of thinking. A time will come when those who cling to the materialistic way of thinking will unite with the Moon powers and surround the Earth, which will be a burnt-out corpse, together with the Moon. For all they want is to hold on to the life of the Earth and remain united with it; they do not want to take the right course, which is to progress from the Earth's corpse to what will be the future soul and spirit of the Earth."

Michael and Christ Defeat Ahriman

Michael Mystery, Michael's Experiences in the Fulfillment of his Cosmic Mission, Rudolf Steiner, Chapter V, GA 26

"Ahrimanic being's entire form predisposes them to absorb into themselves any kind of intelligence that becomes detached from the Gods. They are suited to assimilate into their own being the entire sum of intellectuality of every kind. Thereby they grow to be the greatest, the most comprehensive and most penetrating Intelligences in the whole Cosmos.

Michael puts the ahrimanic Powers beneath his feet, drives them constantly down into deeper regions, below the one where Man is pursuing his development. Michael, with his foot upon the Dragon, thrusting him into the abyss—such is the stupendous picture, as it lives within human consciousness, of these deeds in the super-sensible world. Through Christ's great sacrifice He will live in the same sphere where Ahriman dwells. Man will have the choice between Christ and Ahriman. The world will be able in mankind's evolution to find the way of Christ."

The Ahrimanic Defeat

A Picture of Earth-Evolution in the Future, Rudolf Steiner, Dornach, May 13, 1921, GA 204

"Whereas in the days of old Atlantis human beings came down to the Earth from Saturn, Jupiter, Mars, and so on—that is to say, beings of soul were drawn into the realm of Earth-existence—since the end of the seventies of last century, other Beings—not of the human order—have been descending to the Earth for the purposes of their further development. From cosmic realms beyond the Earth, they come down to the Earth and enter into a definite relationship with human beings. Since the eighties of the nineteenth century, super-Earthly Beings have been seeking to enter the sphere of Earth-existence. Just as the Vulcan-men were the last to come down to the Earth so now Vulcan Beings are actually coming into the realm of Earthly existence. Super-Earthly Beings are already here, and the fact that we are able to have a connected body of Spiritual Science at all today is due to the circumstance that Beings from beyond the Earth are bringing the messages from the spiritual world down into Earth-existence.

Spiritual Beings are seeking to come down into Earth-existence and ought to be willingly received. Catastrophe after catastrophe must ensue, and Earthly life will fall at length into social chaos, if opposition is maintained in human existence to the advent of these Beings. They desire nothing else than to be the advance-guards of what will happen to Earth-existence when the Moon is once again united with the Earth.

These Beings of whom I have spoken will gradually come down to the Earth. Vulcan Beings, 'Supermen' of Vulcan, 'Supermen' of Venus, of Mercury, of the Sun, will unite with this Earth-existence. But if human beings persist in nothing but opposition to them, Earth-existence will pass over into chaos over the next few thousand years.

And from the Earth there will spring forth a terrible brood of beings, a brood of automata of an order of existence lying between the mineral and the plant kingdoms and possessed of an overwhelming power of intellect. This swarm will seize upon the Earth, will spread over the Earth like a network of ghastly, spider-like creatures, of an order lower than that of plant-existence, but possessed of overpowering wisdom. These spidery creatures will be all interlocked with one another, and in their outward movements they will imitate the thoughts that men have spun out of the shadowy intellect that has not allowed itself to be quickened by the new form of Imaginative Knowledge by Spiritual Science. All the thoughts that lack substance and reality will then be endowed with being.

The Earth will be surrounded—as it is now with air and as it sometimes is with swarms of locusts—with a brood of terrible spider-like creatures, half-mineral, half-plant, interweaving with masterly intelligence, it is true, but with intensely evil intent. And in so far as man has not allowed his shadowy intellectual concepts to be quickened to life, his existence will be united not with the Beings who have been trying to descend since the last third of the nineteenth century, but with this ghastly brood of half-mineral, half-plant like creatures. He will have to live together with these spider-like creatures and to continue his cosmic existence within the order of evolution into which this brood will then enter.

The issue at stake is whether human beings will resolve in the present epoch to make themselves worthy to receive what the good Spirits who want to unite with men are bringing down from the Cosmos, or whether men intend to seek their future cosmic existence within the tangled, spider-brood of their own shadowy thoughts. And the concrete reality is that the intellectual thoughts evolved inwardly by men today will in time to come creep over the Earth like a spider's web wherein human beings will be enmeshed, if they will not reach out to a world lying beyond and above their shadowy thoughts and concepts.

A form of knowledge must develop which produces quite a different conception of the being of man, and it can be developed only by raising science to the level of artistic perception. We shall realize then that science as it is today capable of grasping only the mineral nature, whether in the mineral kingdom itself or in the kingdoms of plant, animal, and man. And until we realize that Nature is a world of creative art which can be understood only through artistic feeling, no healing will come into our picture of the world.

It is not right for the shadowy intellect to be driven down into an order of existence lower than that of the plants, into the brood of spidery creatures that will spread over the Earth. Man's being needs to have reached a higher level of existence when, in the eighth millennium, women will become barren, and the Moon will unite once again with the Earth. The Earthly must then remain behind, with man directing and controlling it from outside like an object which he need not carry over with him into cosmic existence. Man must so prepare himself that he need not be involved in what must inevitably develop upon the surface of the Earth in this way.

Intellect will then be objectivized in the very limbs and tentacles of these spidery creatures, who in all their wonderful inter-weavings and caduceus-like convolutions will present an amazing network of intricate forms.

It is only by developing an inner understanding for what is truly artistic that man will be able to understand the realm that is higher than mineral existence—that realm of which we see an expression in the actual shaping and form of the surfaces of things in the world."

Mechanical Occultism

To comprehend the being Ahriman, we need to know his current activities and create a picture of what he will be doing in the near and distant future. Lucifer's time is past, and his many gifts and hindrances are known. Lucifer will not incarnate again. Ahriman, on the other hand, has already incarnated in North America and wishes to live forever in a human body augmented and supplemented by mechanical means. He uses the forces of electricity and electromagnetism to create a realm that exists somewhere between the mineral and plant kingdoms. This new realm is constantly abuzz with machines powered by electricity. The electric wires crisscrossing the landscape are the spider-network where the cold-hearted, grey, dead thoughts of humans are captured and work against the spiritual development of humanity. It is our unconscious participation in this spider-network of non-human sub-nature that gives Ahriman a realm in which to rule during his incarnation. This is the in-between realm where we will find mechanical occultism, mechanical materialism, and machine intelligence. When we use this ahrimanic kingdom without consciousness, our souls are in peril.

There are four elements and four ethers that can help us picture how Ahriman accomplishes mechanical occultism. Warmth (fire) is the element and ether that Ahriman turns to cold-hearted thinking instead of the "warmed-up thoughts" that Steiner tells us to develop for spiritual advancement. Light ether (air) is essentially electro-static energy that permeates all matter and the Cosmos. Ahriman takes this light and turns it into dark shadow-thinking, which is an activity devoid of true light and one that engenders the thought that humans are nothing more than evolved animals. As light "falls into matter," it becomes electricity held in stasis by the form of the matter it is manifesting through. Essentially, all matter is slowed down electricity.

Sound (fluid) or chemical ether creates magnetism, just as electricity running through wires also creates magnetism. Sound ether is again "pulled" out of the ethers and held prisoner in electric wires until it is discharged by its use in devices that require electricity. In electricity, Angels are pulled down into matter.

In electromagnetism, Archangels are pulled down into a type of slavery and enchantment that serves the willpower of humans. Electricity and electromagnetism are forces that insinuate the "beings" behind them.

Life ether (solid) is also pulled down to the Earth and imprisons Archai in the "third force", which is beyond the first two sub-nature forces of electricity and electromagnetism. Rudolf Steiner calls this, the "third force" and describes it as a power beyond anything humanity has known before.

Ahriman, as the ruler of the forces of death, pulls down the Angels, Archangels, and Archai into devices that essentially are the slaves of humanity. Very few people are aware of what electricity is or where it comes from. Just as there are nature forces, there are also sub-nature forces. Ahriman finds his lifeblood in electromagnetic systems and is most interested in developing the "third force" into devices that will have tremendous power. John Worrell Keely developed some devices that worked on vibration and resonance that Rudolf Steiner said were essentially the prototypes of machines that use the "third force." The "third force" can also be used to create healing devices that run on resonant frequencies and harmonics.

All aspects of mechanical workings feed Ahriman and can take away the freedom of humans by supplying electromagnetic slave labor, of which we are we are neither conscious nor thankful. As the forces of death are turned into the "work" that sustains our lives, we need to be aware of the sacrifices of higher hierarchical beings that offer themselves selflessly for our physical labor and our spiritual advancement. Ahriman and his mechanical occultism should not be feared but should be studied carefully to understand how technology can be used for good. We need to realize that Ahriman may have power in this physical world, but he cannot come close to the spirit without burning in pain.

Internet and computer use, as well as all other electronic media, is the home of Ahriman. Many illnesses have been discovered that arise from addiction to the Internet, video games, television, and other electronic apparatus. The Internet can make the user feel almost omniscient and omnipresent as search engines deliver far-reaching knowledge and images to a hand-held device. Ahriman is lulling consciousness into sleep by replacing education with entertainment that dulls the senses and paralyzes living thinking. Soon, only grey spider-thoughts fill the mind of the Internet addicted social media user.

We see that a great deal of what is presented in media are fabricated lies created to detour the thinker into a mire of confusion and anti-social behaviors. Ahriman wants to lull us to sleep through bright lights (Lucifer) and the mechanical miracles of computing and the Internet (Ahriman) so that we slowly lose all hope of finding the spirit through our own higher thinking, feeling, and willing. Ahriman's machines make us lazy, and we eventually lose the ability to think independently or to have any spiritual thoughts that go beyond material sense perception. After a while, ahrimanic possession captures the thinking of the unwitting user.

The answer to Ahriman's seduction into cold-hearted, godless materialism, that makes each person feel like the king of his own kingdom, is the development of a spiritual cosmology that is alive with the wisdom of the hierarchical beings who stand behind outer sense perception. This cosmology will help each person understand who they are and what the human being's goal in evolution is. It will provide the background of spiritual creation (cosmogenesis) and the history of humanity (anthropogenesis) and point in the direction of human evolution. The rightful place of Lucifer, Ahriman, Sorat, and Christ is the foundation of a complete cosmology that places the human being at the center of spiritual evolution.

Cosmology will bring meaning and purpose into the aspirant's life and will help in developing a language of the spirit that can communicate with beings above and below us. Cosmology is the answer to the ahrimanization of the world through materialism and unconscious use of sub-natural forces. Cosmology gives us insight and wisdom so that we can consciously work with Ahriman's tools, transforming grey, dull thinking into thoughts of Moral Imagination, Inspiration, and Intuition.

The Third Force

Rudolf Steiner's audiences of his time were familiar, through theosophical literature, with the inventor John Worrell Keely who was active in America during the second half of the nineteenth century. Keely introduced his "motor," which depended on raising certain vibrations to ever-higher frequencies. It was, however, governed by mechanical vibrations regulated by the inventor himself. In Keely's writings there are accounts of cylinders which released tremendous forces of a mechanical kind, and of vibrators for shattering rocks, useful in the mining industry. There are whole tables of frequencies which affect various spheres of reality. All this was first published by the Theosophical Society and afterwards arranged in book form by one of Keely's sponsors.

Rudolf Steiner shows that electricity and magnetism are related in their fundamental nature to human willpower. At the same time, he emphasizes that these forces are not—like other natural forces—morally neutral, and he warns us of their inherent dangers. After developing this theme further, Steiner said: "For this reason, most occultists did not think it likely that Keely's discoveries would have results in the commercial sense of the word."

Another indication is that this force Keely was working with is suited to powering the largest ship, just as well as a sewing-machine. The "Strader machines" in Steiner's *Mystery Plays* intended to transform social life by enabling everybody to use this power for his own convenience in the home he has designs, according to his own ideas.

The situation of the inventor, Strader, is of special interest. First, he discovers the basic possibility of the machine, which "maintains itself but cannot set itself going." The technical realization of the idea miscarries; and the inventor is finally plunged into an agony of doubt about the basis of his work through the interference of an ahrimanicly inspired know-it-all. How he surmounts this crisis shortly before his death marks an important turning-point in the fourth play of Steiner's, *The Soul's Awakening*.

After briefly indicating that electricity in the Earth-processes of the Post-Atlantean age is "fallen light," and that chemical force transformed in the course of the Earth's evolution, is magnetism, Steiner describes a "third force" which "will influence civilization in an even more wonderful way."

The Nature of Electricity

Concerning Electricity, Rudolf Steiner, Dornach, January 28, 1923, GA 220

"The more we make use of this power (electricity) the more will the Earth tend to become a corpse so that the spiritual part of the Earth can be preparing itself for the Jupiter stage. Forces have to be used to destroy the Earth so that man may be freed from the Earth and the body of the Earth can fall away. As long as the Earth was developing in a forward direction this did not happen for the great civilizing achievements of electricity can serve only a disintegrating Earth. However strange this may sound today; it must be gradually made known. There is an even more terrifying force which cannot be kept secret much longer. We can only hope that when this force comes, as it quite certainly will, a force we have to think of as far more powerful than the strongest electrical charges—we must hope that before any inventor bestows this power on mankind, nothing un-moral will be left in human nature!"

Technical Science and Ahriman

Technology and Art, Their Bearing on Modern Culture,
Rudolf Steiner, Dornach, December 28, 1914, GA 275

"The spiritual beings we have now enticed into our machinery belong to the hierarchy of ahrimanic spirits. A real understanding of modern life makes it evident that through the milieu of applied technical science we pass into an ahrimanic sphere and allow ourselves to be filled with ahrimanic spirituality. Nobody can say with truth that he is protecting himself from Ahriman, for there are no means whereby he could do so. It is only because in the present incarnation we are obliged to live in the milieu created by technical science that it is possible to come into connection with the ahrimanic spirituality, into connection with what in earlier incarnations could be submerged in a more essentially artistic element. In this way we set over against certain luciferic forces the ahrimanic forces of today, and so we establish a balance, whereas formerly the pendulum of life swung now to the one side, now to the other."

Keely Vibratory Energy

Origin and Goal of the Human Being, The Future of the Human Being, Rudolf Steiner, Lecture XVIII, Berlin, March, 1905, GA 53

"New ideals arise just in the most excellent spirits. Indeed, these spirits who point to a distant future are not the so-called practical spirits, but the world history advances differently than the practical people fancy it. I have pointed to a pillar of idealism, to Tolstoy before. Today, however, I would still like to point to a western spirit, to Keely (John Ernst Worrell Keely 1827-1898, inventor of a motor based on "vibratory energy") the great mechanic who furthers us although his mechanical idea is not yet a practical one. Some questions are connected with it which may appear fantastic to the materialist. But at the same time, we want to get to know an idealism that is of another type than that of the everyday life. It is the same that lived in the mysteries once."

Moral Machines

The Temple Legend, The Royal Art in a New Form, Rudolf Steiner, Berlin, Lecture XX, January 2, 1906, GA 93

"It is perhaps known to you that Keely invented a motor which would only go if he himself were present. He was not deceiving people about this; for he had in him that driving force originating in the soul, which can set machines in motion. A driving force which can only be moral, that is the idea of the future; a most important force, with which culture must be inoculated, if it is not to fall back on itself. The mechanical and the moral must interpenetrate each other, because the mechanical is nothing without the moral. Today we stand hard on this frontier. In the future machines will be driven not only by water and steam, but by spiritual force, by spiritual morality. This power is symbolized by the Tau sign and was indeed poetically symbolized by the image of the Holy Grail."

Machines and Ahrimanic Forces

Three Streams in the Evolution of Mankind, Rudolf Steiner, Lecture V, December 10, 1918, GA 184

"By learning to understand the rhythms in nature we shall even come to a certain application of the rhythmical in technology. This would be the goal for future technology: harmoniously related vibrations would be set going; they would be small at first but would act upon each other so that they became larger and larger, and by this means, simply through their resonance, a tremendous amount of work could be done."

Sympathetic Vibrations

Man as Symphony of the Creative Word, Rudolf Steiner, Lecture II, October 20, 1923, GA 230

"The whole way in which people construct machines varies greatly according to the nature of the machine in question; but everything tends towards the gradual development of these still imperfect, primitive machines into a kind of machine which depends upon vibrations, and where the aim is to make the machines effective by means of vibrations or oscillations, by means of movements which run a periodic course. Everything is hastening towards such machines. But if once these machines in their coordinated activity could be constructed in such a way as can be learned from the distribution of foodstuffs in the organization of the cow, then the vibrations which would be conjured up on the Earth-globe through the machines, these small Earth-vibrations, would so run their course that what is above the Earth would sound together with, vibrate together with what is happening on the Earth; so that our planetary system in its movements would be compelled to vibrate with our Earth-system, just as a string tuned to a certain pitch vibrates in sympathy when another one is struck in the same room.

That is the terrible law of the sounding in unison of vibrations which would be fulfilled if the alluring call of the cow would so decoy the orient that it would then be able to penetrate in an absolutely convincing way into the unspiritual, purely mechanistic civilization of the west and center, and thereby it would become possible to conjure up on the Earth a mechanistic system fitting exactly into the mechanistic system of the universe. Through this everything connected with the working of air, with the forces of the circumference, and everything connected with the working of the stars, would be exterminated from human civilization. What man experiences, for instance, through the cycle of the year, what he experiences through living together with the sprouting, budding life of spring, with the fading, dying life of autumn—all this would lose its import for him. Human civilization would resound with the clattering and rattling of the vibrating machines and with the echo of this clattering and rattling which would stream down upon the Earth from the Cosmos as a reaction to this mechanization of the Earth. A part of our present-day civilization is actually on the way to having this terrible element of degeneracy as its goal."

Mechanical Demons

The Karma of Vocation, Rudolf Steiner, November 27, 1916, GA 172

"When the steam engine is created in this way, Ahriman gains the possibility of establishing himself as a demon even in the very physical entity. In constructing steam engines, the condition is created for the incarnation of demons. If anyone is unwilling to believe in them, he need not do so; that is negative superstition. Positive superstition consists in seeing spirits where there are none; negative superstition consists in denying spirits where they are. In steam engines, ahrimanic demons are actually brought even into a physical object. That is, while the Cosmos has descended with its spiritual element through what has been poured into human evolution, the spirit of the Cosmos is driven out through what is created in the form of demons. That is to say, this new, important and wonderful advance has brought about not only a demonology, but also a demon magic that frequently imbues modern technology."

Electricity and Magnetism

The Wrong and Right Use of Esoteric Knowledge,
Rudolf Steiner, Lecture III, November 25, 1917, GA 178

"One of these great problems will be concerned with finding out how to place the spiritual etheric forces at the service of practical life. I have told you that in this epoch we have to solve the problem of how the radiations from human states of mind are carried over into machines; of how human beings are to be brought into relation with an environment which must become increasingly mechanised. The welding together of human beings with machines will be a great and important problem for the rest of the Earth-evolution.

Human consciousness depends on destructive forces. In our nerve-system we are always in the process of dying. These forces of death will become stronger and stronger, and we shall find that they are related to the forces of electricity and magnetism, and to those at work in machines. A man will be able in a certain sense to guide his intentions and his thoughts into the forces of the machines. Forces in human nature that are still unknown will be discovered—forces which will act upon external electricity and magnetism. That is one problem: the bringing together of human beings with machines, and this is something which will exert ever-increasing influence on the future."

Asuras and the Eighth Sphere

From the Contents of Esoteric Classes, Rudolf Steiner, GA 266

"Asuras are spirits of the very greatest egoism who remained behind during Saturn evolution. They want to condense matter and compress it ever more so that it can't be spiritualized and brought back to its original condition. They're the dregs of the planetary evolution that goes form Saturn to Vulcan. The Asuras inhabit the Moon and from there they work on the men whom they want to drag down into the eighth sphere and thereby tear away from progressive evolution and its goal—the Christ. All those who strive towards the eighth sphere will eventually live on a moon."

Sorat and the Eighth Sphere

Reading the Pictures of the Apocalypse, Rudolf Steiner, May 21, 1909, Kristiania, Lecture XII, GA 104a

"But those who have proven themselves to be immature in the age of Venus-Earth, who have placed themselves under the rulership of Sorat, must now isolate themselves on a special sphere of Earth while the other seven proceed downward and again upward. Thus, the colony of Sorat falls away. The black magicians inhabit this Eighth Sphere, which goes to the left and away, and the beast gives a home to all that thus falls away: that is the Eighth Sphere. In this way we can find all the teachings of Theosophy in the Apocalypse."

Ahriman and the Eighth Sphere

The Occult Movement in the Nineteenth Century, Rudolf Steiner, Lecture V, October 18, 1915, GA 254

"There are not many words that can be used for characterizing the Eighth Sphere. The Eighth Sphere cannot be anything that belongs to the material world. It has something to do with the residue left from the Old Moon and its evolution. The Eighth Sphere is found by way of visionary Imaginations. Here, then, we have a sphere, visible only to visionary-imaginative clairvoyance, which stands there as an Eighth Sphere over and above the seven which constitute the domain of the ordered and regular evolution of mankind.

The Eighth Sphere is a realm in which we are living all the time. In the Eighth Sphere we have to do with Imaginations, and what constitutes the essential nature of Earth-evolution is not present in the Eighth Sphere. The mineral element is totally absent from the Eighth Sphere.

Instead of pure Imaginations being there, the Imaginations are densified by the infusion of a mineral element that has been wrested from the Earth. Densified Imaginations are thus created. They are ghosts, spectres—that is to say, behind our world there is a world of spectres created by Lucifer and Ahriman.

To the seven Spheres, an eighth, created in opposition to the progressive Spirits, has been added. The necessary consequence of this is that the Spirits of Form must do battle on the Earth for every morsel of substantiality capable of mineralization, lest it should be wrested from them by Lucifer and Ahriman and born into the Eighth Sphere.

Lucifer and Ahriman strive unceasingly to draw from the Earth's substances whatever they can snatch, in order to form their Eighth Sphere which then, when it is sufficiently advanced, will be detached from the Earth and go its own way in the Cosmos together with Lucifer and Ahriman. Needless to say, the Earth would then pass over to Future Jupiter as a mere torso. Therefore, we ourselves are involved in the battle. Lucifer and Ahriman battle against the Spirits of Form, with the aim of wresting mineral substance from us everywhere. Lucifer and Ahriman from the beginning of Earth-evolution want to let the whole of this evolution disappear into the Eighth Sphere. It was therefore necessary that a counterweight should be created by those Spirits who belong to the Hierarchy of the Spirits of Form.

Care had to be taken that not everything in man proceeding from the head can become the prey of Lucifer and Ahriman; that not everything shall depend upon head-activity and the activity of the outward-turned senses, for then Lucifer and Ahriman would have been victors. It was necessary that a counterweight should be created in the domain of Earthly life, that there should be in the human being something entirely independent of the head. And this was achieved through the work of the good Spirits of Form, who implanted the principle of Love into the principle of heredity on Earth.

From this you will understand that what stems from the free will must be kept within the realm of Earth. This means that man is perpetually exposed to the danger of having his free will wrested from him and dragged by Lucifer and Ahriman into the Eighth Sphere.

Lucifer and Ahriman are engaged perpetually in shackling man's free will and in conjuring all sorts of things before him in order to tear away what he makes out of these things and let it disappear in the Eighth Sphere.

When clairvoyance in all kinds of different forms develops in naive, credulous, superstitious people, it is often the case that their free will has been sacrificed. Then Lucifer instantly seizes hold of it, and whereas these people imagine they have had an experience of immortality, the truth is that in their visions they see a part, or a product, of their souls being wrested away and prepared for the Eighth Sphere."

Cosmological Antidotes for Mechanical Occultism

Cosmology is the antidote to mechanical occultism because it builds a comprehensive world view that changes the perspective of the viewer. If your cosmology is spiritual, you will see spirit beings. If your cosmology is materialistic, you will see only matter. Our worldview is the lens that turns perceptions into concepts. Each person's concepts are unique even though what we perceive is essentially the same. Basically, we project our concepts onto perception and thus see what we are looking to find. For instance, before 2101 BC, there were few words for war and thus there was very little war. Some cultures had no weapons and no words for war and consequently knew nothing of war. There was no concept of war, hence, no war.

If you believe in the Big Bang and the subsequent "entropy until death", then don't expect a life full of living, creative spiritual beings to have a place in your worldview (cosmology). It truly is that simple. If you believe in the spiritual world, then you will ultimately find spiritual beings.

A cosmology informs a person where they came from, where they are, and where they are going. In other words, it places the person in an intelligently designed scheme that has a goal in space and time. Once the personal perspective has a strong foundation, a cosmology will then connect the aspirant to the forces, beings, and consciousness behind the physical world. You discover your roots in the spirit and learn about the spiritual home awaiting your return. The entire cyclic process of birth, death, and rebirth is spelled out in a true cosmology so that the dignity of the human being in the larger scheme of the Cosmos is central.

We are important beings in the grand scheme of the divine plan, not insignificant creatures in an unfathomable universe. We are cut from the same cosmic fabric as the gods, and like them, we are immortal. This is the faith and confidence that a true cosmology gives the seeker. To know who you are and what stage of development you are currently living in, and to have knowledge that reincarnation makes you immortal can bring great comfort and peace. A confidence develops in the soul that has developed a spiritual cosmology that supports clear thinking and self-development.

Mechanical occultism, the tool of Ahriman which will become the outer garment of his incarnation, enslaves the willpower of those who use it without understanding. We can see this happening in the unconscious use of electricity, which creates our modern life. Who understands electricity? We can forge it to our uses, but we do not understand it. Even more so with mechanical occultism, which has much broader effects upon humans and the planet. But if we can bring consciousness and understanding to these ahrimanic insights, we can use the forces of mechanical occultism for the benefit of humanity. Evil only lasts "for a time" and then it falls back into the stream of progressive beings or devolves into sub-nature. Therefore, the resonant vibrations of mechanical occultism are being developed right now and are passing through us all the time. Our job is to develop the consciousness that finds the proper place for those forces and understands the ways that they can be used for good.

Mechanical occultism is basically the black magic practice of taking the "harmony of the spheres", the vibrations the Sun and planets make in the ethers, and turning them into weapons against humanity. These same forces are also the waves, frequencies, and energies that hierarchical beings create when they come into manifestation, like a 3D object casting a 2D shadow. These cosmic vibrations and undulating energies are the shadows of Angels falling into matter for the sustenance of human beings. Harmonic cosmic waves, or celestial music, resonate with our bodily organs to nourish them as they evolve into new super-sensible organs of perception able to see into the spiritual world.

Rudolf Steiner calls the deepest sub-nature force, the "third force", which can be used for good or ill depending on the level of consciousness of the person using it. Materialistic scientists will see it as a weapon or a force to manipulate the movement of the planets and other heavenly bodies. Spiritual people, who have developed a sound cosmology, will see it as heavenly music that opens new spiritual capacities for them to see higher realms. The disparity between them exists in the perception of the beholder, which is enhanced by morality and diminished by immorality.

If humanity could create a living cosmology that adds morality to the scientific use of this "third force", we could solve all the energy problems on the globe. The movement of planets and the true forces of the Sun hold the keys to new energy sources. Materialistic, sense-bound scientists will discover the "third force", but then try to manipulate it through their usual processes of analysis and destruction that lead to entropy and cosmic death. Science only sees what it can disassemble with numbers, measurements, weight, and transient theories. Some reasonable scientists may marvel at the living forces of levity, but since they can't control or dissect them, they give up on any further investigation of their nature or source. Materialistic science leads to a tunnel-vision view of reality that can't see the true nature of the forces used by the spirit to create our visible world from the invisible worlds.

A living cosmology leads us to understanding embryology, according to Rudolf Steiner. The microcosm is mirrored in the macrocosm, "as above so below." The forces in the West lead us to mechanical occultism and the death mysteries, the use of eugenics in the East lead us to the birth mysteries. As death comes to meet birth, mechanical occultism meets eugenics; the circle is complete. Steiner told us that "by necessity" the East must meet the West so that the full life cycle of birth and death might become complete. Eugenics controls the soul who is born into the world while mechanical occultism leads it towards a meaningless death. In between, the seeker needs to develop a cosmology that can answer questions of eugenics and mechanical occultism through the life-giving mysteries of hygienic occultism, which is developed by the heart forces of the middle ground of Europe. Cosmology enables the aspirant to see that life should not be bound by either extreme occult force, because the faith and wisdom of human immortality encompasses both cosmological concerns of where we came from (pre-birth) and where we are going (after death). Hygienic occultism, as the middle ground, is found through Christ in the rhythmic heart forces of breath and blood. These are the forces of love that can bind together the East and West in a healthy, living fashion.

The need for the West to study the East and the East to study the West is imperative in our times. The solutions for mechanical occultism lie within the wisdom of the East and vice versa. It is not by coincidence that Nikola Tesla, an extraordinarily free spirit both spiritually and scientifically, kept company of some the greatest Eastern mystics of his day, including Swami Vivekananda.

Rudolf Steiner tells us in his book, *Philosophy, Cosmology and Religion*, that "man not only needs a philosophy; he needs a cosmology." Every person needs to understand how he belongs to the Cosmos and to what extent he has evolved out of the Cosmos. Ancient humanity felt the Cosmos as a whole but modern scientists separate the parts of the Cosmos into dying forces of nature and only recognize laws of physical sensory phenomena that they imagine hold them together. That limited worldview will only provide understanding about the physical body of the human being but not the soul. To arrive at a comprehensive cosmology, we need a knowledge of the etheric and astral aspects of the human being also. To have a working cosmology, we must recognize the archetype of the human being with soul-spiritual capacities aligned with the etheric and astral bodies, alongside of the physical body and the overarching ego (I Am).

In the past, religious life flowed into a person as a perception that was philosophical, theological, and cosmological. In religious experience, the person was united with the divine world and this experience was the highest form of perceptual life, a sort of natural clairvoyance with the creator beings of nature. What we need in our time is a modern philosophy developed from an exact clairvoyant knowledge of the ether body—a cosmology that includes the central role of humanity through a complete understanding of the etheric and astral organisms and a renewal of religious life through an exact clairvoyant understanding of the true nature of the human ego, or I consciousness, which exists beyond waking and sleeping.

To develop an effective cosmology, one's meditative life must be extended to interaction with the living archetypes found in the cosmology. The aspirant must be able to concentrate totally on certain concepts in full wakefulness and consciousness devoid of any soul content derived from the senses, or from thinking itself. The soul must become awake and have within itself nothing of the content acquired through ordinary daytime consciousness. Once this is done, cosmic content can flow into this anxious seeking vessel of the soul, beckoning to the spiritual world. This experience and interaction with the spiritual world are called the stage of Moral Inspiration, which follows the stage of super-sensible perception called Moral Imagination.

We can also see the Cosmos in its fundamental, lawful order manifesting in the human body's rhythmic processes of breathing and blood circulation. We can arrive at a cosmology by which the astral organism and the rhythmic processes in each individual person are understood and developed into Moral Technique, as Steiner called it.

Imaginal, intuitive inspirations become the source of a genuine, modern cosmology that is on par with ancient comprehensive cosmologies. Humanity's ancient dream-like forces of soul made them a member of the whole Cosmos, of a soul-spiritual cosmic world. The knowledge gained in intuitively inspired perception should be acquired in full consciousness and reflected in the etheric body, unlike the natural clairvoyance of the ancients. Moral Inspirations project themselves in pictures upon the etheric body. The insight gained through inspiration from the Cosmos connects with the creation of picture-making in the activity of the etheric body. What is inspired out of the Cosmos is inwardly in motion and cannot at once be brought into sharp outlines. This only happens when it links itself with the experiences of imagination and inspiration in the ether body. Then, cosmology can be brought into sharp outlines whereby a cosmic philosophy arises completely appropriate for modern humanity, a philosophical cosmology, which is formed through a flowing together of inspired knowledge with the imaginations experienced pictorially in the ether body.

If you are able to formulate in concepts and ideas what has been attained through inspired cognition by letting it stream back into ordinary consciousness, you arrive at a true cosmology that encompasses the whole of human and cosmic evolution. Such a cosmology then, is an experienced cosmology. We can say that when this stage of inspiration during sleep is consciously reflected back, humanity learns to recognize itself as a member of the cosmic order – a cosmic order that is expressed in a planetary sense as a cosmic ordering of natural law.

To relive in our soul in full consciousness an earlier epoch of humanity's evolution in which the process of breathing could become a process of perception, is the prerequisite for a modern cosmology. Cosmology as a spiritual science can only be established if it is given its content from spiritual perception. One can no longer arrive at content by deduction. To attain a content of cosmology one must borrow from ancient clairvoyant perceptions. If we wish to advance beyond a naturalistic cosmology to a new one that embraces humanity's totality, we must learn to perceive with the aid of inspiration and intuition, that element in humanity in which the spiritual Cosmos is reflected. We must use imagination, inspiration, and intuition to construct a genuinely real cosmology.

This insight points us in the direction for a healing cosmology that can also incorporate sub-nature and the future states of human consciousness. Any cosmology useful to the future evolution of humanity must also include the central deed of evolution—the Mystery of Golgotha. Christ is the key to a cosmology that places humanity in the dynamic between Lucifer and Ahriman. It is the gift of ego consciousness that can stand in the middle path between these adversarial forces and find a true cosmology based upon the gift of Christ.

Eugenic, Hygienic and Mechanical Occultism

The Challenge of the Times: The Mechanistic, Eugenic and Hygienic Aspects of the Future, Rudolf Steiner, Lecture III, December 1, 1918, GA 186

"This threefold capacity, of which every knowing person within these secret circles speaks—these three capacities that will evolve in human nature, I must make intelligible to you in the following way. First, there are the capacities having to do with so-called mechanical occultism. By means of this capacity—and this is precisely the ideal of British secret societies—certain social forms at present basic within the industrial system shall be set up on an entirely different foundation. Every knowing member of these secret circles is aware that, solely by means of certain capacities that are still latent but evolving in man, and with the help of the law of harmonious oscillations, machines and mechanical constructions and other things can be set in motion. A small indication is to be found in what I connected with the person of Strader in my *Mystery Dramas*.

These things are at present in process of development. They are guarded as secrets within those secret circles in the field of mechanical occultism. Motors can be set in motion, into activity, by an insignificant human influence through a knowledge of the corresponding curve of oscillation. By means of this principle it will be possible to substitute merely mechanical forces for human forces in many things. The possibility will thus come about of rendering unnecessary nine-tenths of the work of individuals within the regions of the English-speaking peoples. Mechanistic occultism will not only render it possible to do without nine-tenths of the labour still performed at present by human hands but will give the possibility also of paralyzing every uprising attempted by the then dissatisfied masses of humanity.

The capacity to set motors in motion according to the laws of reciprocal oscillations will develop on a great scale among the English-speaking peoples. This is known in their secret circles and is counted upon as the means whereby the mastery over the rest of the population of the Earth shall be achieved even in the course of the Fifth Post-Atlantean Epoch. Something else is known also in those circles. It is known that there are two other capacities that will likewise develop. One, which I shall venture to call the eugenic occultism (capacity), will evolve primarily among people of the East, of Russia and the Asiatic hinterland. It is also known in those secret circles of the West that this eugenic occultism will not evolve out of the inborn potentialities of the English-speaking peoples, but only of the inborn potentialities belonging precisely to the Asiatic and the Russian populations. These facts are known in the secret circles of the West. They are taken into account and are looked upon as constituting certain motive forces that must become active in future evolution.

By the eugenic capacity I mean the removal of the reproduction of human beings from the sphere of mere arbitrary impulse and accident. Among the peoples of the East there will gradually develop a brilliantly clear knowledge as to how the laws of population, the laws of peopling the Earth, must run parallel with certain cosmic phenomena. From this information they will know that, if conception is brought about in accord with certain constellations of the stars, opportunities will thus be given for souls that are either good or evil in their natures to obtain access for Earthly incarnation. This capacity will be acquired only by those individuals who constitute the continuation as races, the continuation in the blood stream, of the Asiatic population. They will be able simply to see in detail how what works today chaotically and arbitrarily in conception and birth can be brought into harmony with the great laws of the Cosmos in individual concrete cases. Here abstract laws are of no avail. What will be acquired is a concrete single capacity in which it will be known in individual cases whether or not a conception should occur at a particular time.

This knowledge, which will make it possible to bring down from the heavens the impelling forces for the moralizing or demoralizing of the Earth through the nature of man himself, this special capacity evolves as a continuation of the blood capacity in the races of the East. What evolves as a capacity there I call eugenic occultism. This is the second capacity—the capacity that will prevent the evolution of humanity as regards conception and birth from taking its course according to arbitrary impulses, and more or less accidentally.

The American occultists know that they can never carry over into the future what they will to carry over unless they nurture what will develop in the form of bodies for the future within the Russian population through its eugenic occult potentialities, unless they gain the mastery of this, so that a social union can gradually come into existence between their own decadent race characteristics and the germinating psychic race characteristics of European Russia. We have all three: the mechanical occult capacity, the eugenic occult capacity, and the hygienic occult capacity. This capacity will come to maturity simply through the insight that human life, in its course from birth to death, progresses in a manner identical with the process of an illness.

Processes of illnesses are, in other words, only special and radical transmutations of the quite ordinary, normal life process taking its course between birth and death, except that we bear within ourselves not only the forces that create illness but also those that heal. These healing forces are precisely the same as those that are applied when a person acquires occult capacities, in which case these forces are transmuted into the forces of knowledge. The healing power innate in the human organism, when transmuted into knowledge, gives occult forms of knowledge.

Materialistic medicine will have no basis in the future. As soon as the hygienic occult capacities evolve, a person will need no external material medicine, but the possibility will exist of treating prophylactically in a psychic way to prevent those illnesses that do not arise through karmic causes because karmic illnesses cannot be influenced. Now, the situation is such that these three faculties will not come into existence equally among all the peoples of the Earth. It is precisely in the West that these will be applied, but the manner in which they will be applied will be that a mastery will be established over the Eastern lands, and marriages will be brought about between people of the West and people of the East. Thus, use will be made of what can be learned only from the people of the East.

The East and those of the Central countries will have to receive mechanical occultism from the West. They will receive its benefits, its products. Hygienic occultism will develop primarily in the Central countries, and eugenic occultism in the Eastern lands. It will be necessary, however, for inter-communication to exist between people."

Cosmology in the West

Cosmogony, Freedom, Altruism, Rudolf Steiner, Dornach, October 10, 1919, GA 191

"We cannot today arrive at the secrets of our civilization, my dear friends, unless we can distinguish how these three impulses needed for its rise are distributed among the different members of our Earth's surface—unless we know that the tendency towards Cosmogony is an endowment of the Anglo-American world, that the tendency towards Freedom lies in the European world; whilst the tendency towards Altruism and towards that temperament which, properly realized, leads to social feeling is, strictly speaking, peculiar to Asiatic culture. America, Europe, Asia, each have one third of what must be attained for any true regeneration, any real reconstruction of our civilization.

At present, this of course comes out, has and does come out, in a curious way. Anglo-American civilization is conquering the world. But, in conquering the world, it will need to absorb what the conquered parts of the world have to give—the impulse to Freedom, the impulse to Altruism; for in itself it has only the impulse to Cosmogony. Indeed, Anglo-American civilization owes its success to a cosmogonic impulse. It owes it to the circumstance that people are able to think in world-thoughts.

The Anglo-American being—a striving towards Cosmogony
The European being—a striving towards Freedom
The Asiatic being—a striving towards Altruism

Anyone acquainted with the spiritual life of the Anglo-American world knows, that formalistic and materialistic as Anglo-American spiritual life is in the first instance—and though indeed it even tries to get to what is spiritual in a materialistic fashion—yet it has in it the makings of a cosmogony. Although this cosmogony is today being sought along altogether erroneous paths, yet it lies in the Anglo-American nature to seek for it. The possibility of bringing this cosmogony into connection with free, altruistic man does not exist. There is the talent for treating this cosmogony as an ornamental appendage, for working it out and giving it shape; but no talent for incorporating the human being in this cosmogony as a member of it. Even the Spiritualist Movement, in its early beginnings in the middle of the nineteenth century (of which it still preserves some traces)—had, one may say, something of a Cosmogony about it, although it led into the wilderness. What they were trying to get at, were the forces that lay behind the sense-forces, only they took a materialistic road, and used materialistic methods, to find them. But they were not endeavouring through these means to arrive at a science of the formalist kind that you get, for instance, among the Europeans. They were trying to become acquainted with the real, super-sensible forces. Only, as I said, they took a wrong road. So, here again, we have one third of what will have to be there before our civilization can re-ascend."

The Sixth Epoch—Goals of the Future

Significant Facts Pertaining to the Spiritual Life of the Middle of the XIXth Century, Rudolf Steiner, Dornach, October 31st, 1915, GA 254

"We are now living in the Fifth Epoch of the First Post-Atlantean Age; then come into the Sixth and Seventh Epochs. During the Sixth and Seventh Epochs, the rigidity of the etheric body will have a great influence upon the physical body and the physical body will become a faithful copy of the etheric. But these things will have no meaning whatever during the Sixth Epoch, our bodily form will then obtain its expression from the series of our incarnations. The human beings will differ very much from one another, and their features will be strongly marked. When we encounter somebody, we shall then know exactly: This is a good person and that is an evil one. The human countenance will thus more and more express the moral qualities.

If our etheric body is to be strong, so that it may be able to correct the mistakes of our physical body, its strength should be evident through the fact that we learn to consider the things which come to us from the etheric world as something very earnest and real. This will be the attitude which will be able to exercise a more and more healing influence. It will be necessary above all that we should take up spiritual science, so as to be prepared for the moment when the etheric shape of Christ shall appear to us, and so that we may take this up with due earnestness and in the right spirit. We face a time in which we shall first of all discover the Christ, and in following Him we shall gradually discover the etheric. Even then, this etheric element will have the strength to make of us individual human beings."

Good and Evil in the Sixth Epoch

Reading the Pictures of the Apocalypse, Cosmogony, Rudolf Steiner, Paris, June 14, 1906, GA 104a

"After our Fifth Epoch another will come, the Sixth, which will be related to ours as a spiritually minded soul is related to a rationally inclined soul. This epoch will bring genius, clairvoyance, the creative spirit, to development. The mechanical science of the physical plane will be elevated to the heights of spiritual creative power. That will be gnosis or spiritual knowledge. This Sixth Epoch will be radically different from ours. Great, tumultuous catastrophes will precede it, for the Sixth Epoch will be just as spiritual as ours is materialistic, but such a transformation can only occur through great, physical upheavals. Everything that will be formed in the course of the Sixth Epoch will call into existence the possibility of a Seventh Epoch which itself will form the end of these post-Atlantean cultures and will know completely different conditions of life from our own. This Seventh Epoch will end with a revolution of the elements, similar to the one that brought an end to the Atlantean continent.

Human beings always carry within themselves what they will see around them in future times. All that presently exists around us actually came forth from us in preceding ages. What human beings possess today as their inner soul life, their thoughts, their feelings, will similarly be revealed externally and become the environment in which people live. The future resides in the hearts of men and women. The choice is ours to decide for a future of good or of evil. Just as it is true that the human being once left behind something that then became the world of animals, so too, what is evil in the human being will one day form a kind of degenerate humanity. At the present time we can more or less hide the good or evil within us. A day will come when we can no longer do this, when the good or the evil will be written indelibly on our forehead, on our body, and even on the face of the Earth. Humanity will then be split into two races. In the same way that we encounter boulders or animals today, in the future we will encounter beings of pure evil and ugliness. When a human being's facial features become an expression of that individual's karma, then people will separate themselves according to the stream in which they apparently belong. Everything depends on whether human beings have conquered the lower nature within them or whether this lower nature has triumphed over the spirit."

Manes and the Sixth Epoch

The Manicheans, Rudolf Steiner, Berlin, November 11, 1904, GA 93

"Manes [Mani] will prepare for that epoch in which the men of the Sixth Epoch will be led by themselves, by the light of their own souls. Manes will create an overlapping stream, a stream which goes further than the stream of the Rosicrucians. The stream of Manes goes over to the Sixth Epoch which has been in preparation since the founding of Christianity. Christianity will appear in its perfected form in the Sixth Epoch.

A number of human beings must be formed into an organization, a form, in which the Christianity of the Sixth Epoch can find its place. In this Sixth Epoch, good and evil will form a far greater contrast than they do today. In the Sixth Epoch, evil will appear, especially in the spiritual. There will be men who are mighty in love and goodness. But evil will also be there as a mood and a disposition without any covering, within a large number of human beings. They will extol evil. The task of the Sixth Epoch is to draw evil again into itself through gentleness. It must express itself in the forming of a community which has to spread above all things: peace, love, and non-resistance to evil."

Characteristics of the Sixth Epoch

Faith, Love, and Hope: Towards the Sixth Epoch, Rudolf Steiner, December 3, 1911, GA 130

"The whole purpose of spiritual science is to prepare in this sense for the Sixth Epoch of culture. Herein we prepare what spiritual science calls freedom of thought. By coming together in friendly associations for the purpose of cultivating spiritual science, we prepare the culture, the civilization of the Sixth Post-Atlantean Epoch.
In the Sixth Epoch:
- the well-being of the individual will depend entirely upon the well-being of the whole,
- the most highly cultured will not only feel pain such as is caused today by the sight of poverty, suffering and misery in the world, but such individuals will experience the suffering of another human being as their own suffering,
- complete freedom of thought and a longing for it will so lay hold of men that what a man likes to believe, what religious convictions

he holds, will rest wholly within the power of his own individuality. Everyone will feel that complete freedom of thought in the domain of religion is a fundamental right of the human being,

- people will only be considered to have real knowledge when they recognize the spiritual, when they know that the spiritual pervades the world and that human souls must unite with the spiritual,
- all materialistic beliefs including science, too, will be regarded as antiquated superstition, Men as a matter of course will accept as science only such forms of knowledge as are based upon the spiritual, upon pneumatology,
- it is the spirit self that must be developed within the souls of men, just as now the consciousness soul is being developed. The nature of spirit self is that it must pre-suppose the existence in human souls of the three characteristics of which I have spoken: social life in which brotherliness prevails, freedom of thought, and pneumatology. These three characteristics are essential in a community of human beings within which the spirit self is to develop as the consciousness soul develops in the souls of the fifth epoch,
- the individual should make preparation for communities into which he will enter entirely of his own free will in the Sixth Epoch. There hovers before us as a high ideal a form of community that will so encompass the Sixth Epoch of culture that civilized human beings will quite naturally meet each other as brothers and sisters,
- Eastern Europe will have to wait until the spirit self comes down to the Earth and can permeate the souls of humanity,
- the Russian soul feels that spirit self is to descend, but that it can only descend into a community of people permeated with the consciousness of brotherhood,
- the spirit of community is needed to bring about the descent of spirit self,
- our aim is to call together human beings who resolve to be brothers and sisters, and above whom hovers something that they strive to develop by cultivating spiritual science, feeling the good spirit of brotherhood hovering over and above them."

Preparing for the Sixth Epoch, The Secret of Death, Rudolf Steiner, Dusseldorf, June 15, 1915, Lecture 13, GA 159

In the Sixth Epoch:

- there will be a reflection within man of the love-nature of the etheric body, and in the seventh, before the great catastrophe, the reflection of the nature of hope of the physical body,
- the need for love will cast its light. Love will show itself in a very different form—different even from that which can be called Christian love. Slowly we draw nearer to that epoch; and by making those in the Anthroposophical Movement familiar with the mysteries of the Cosmos, with the nature of the various individualities both on the physical plane and on the higher planes, we try to kindle love for everything in existence,
- when people grow to realize more and more that the foundations for it are actually within them, and out of their innermost being—in other words, out of love—do what should be done. When forces wake in our souls which impel us to do what we should through love alone, we then discover in us something that must gradually become widespread. Then in a man's nature quite special forces of the etheric body will make themselves known,
- the Bodhisattva's teaching will contain a magical moral force carrying to hearts and souls a full conviction of the eternal, deeply significant brotherhood of intellect and morality. His task will be to enlighten human beings concerning the Mystery of Golgotha. His words will imprint into men's souls directly, magically, the nature of the Mystery of Golgotha,
- the future moral age of man; in a certain sense we could designate it as a coming Golden Age,
- the Christ will gradually reveal Himself to ever-higher powers in human beings,
- teachers will become the interpreters of the great Christ-event for all who are willing to listen,
- through the dawning of the age of love, conditions for the age of morality are prepared,
- we seek for community above us, the living Christ in us."

An Esoteric Cosmology, The Apocalypse, Rudolf Steiner, Lecture XVIII, GA 94

"In the Sixth Epoch:
- mechanical science will become spiritually creative as Gnosis-spiritual consciousness,
- it will be as spiritual as ours has been material,
- humanity will then divide into two races,
- human souls must be strong enough to bring good out of evil by a process of spiritual alchemy."

The Work of Secret Societies in the World, Rudolf Steiner, Berlin, December 23, 1904, GA 93

"In the Sixth Epoch:
- men will understand what the atom is, in reality,
- it will be realized that the atom is nothing but coagulated electricity,
- the attainment of selflessness will enable humanity to be kept from the brink of destruction,
- a tiny handful of selfless humans will make good and insure their survival."

Buddha and Christ, The Sphere of the Bodhisattvas, Rudolf Steiner, Milan, September 21, 1911, GA 130

"The main characteristic of the Sixth Epoch will be:
- what is moral and what is immoral will arise in the souls of men,
- aesthetic pleasure in the good, aesthetic displeasure in the evil,
- immorality will have a paralyzing effect upon intellectuality,
- the number of those able to behold the etheric Christ will steadily increase,
- will have to acquire in the physical world the power to behold the super-sensible Christ,
- Christ comes in an astral body,
- the utterances of the Maitreya Buddha will be permeated with the power of Christ."

The Apocalypse of John, Rudolf Steiner, Lecture VIII, GA 104

"In the Sixth Epoch:

- will proceed people full of understanding for the spiritual world,
- the ripest fruit of our present civilization will appear,
- will bring the spiritual marriage between West and East."

The Battle for the Human Soul

Lucifer drives self-seeking, Ahriman fills the world with lies, and the Asuras pour out soul illness and spiritual death as they try to consume the ego (I Am) of each human being. The human ego is directly assaulted by Sorat, the Sun-Demon, who has entered into human history three times before. In 666 A.D. he worked through the spread of Arabism and scientific materialism; in 1332 he was the inspiration behind the destruction of the Order of the Knights Templar, one of the first groups to understand the Cosmic Christ and His holy mysteries. In 1998, Sorat inspired people who became possessed by him with ravenous evil thoughts, destructive fury in their emotions, and debased animalism in their actions. Even today, these servants of Sorat openly mock and fight against the nourishment of spirit-wisdom and are deeply involved in black magic through worship of Mammon, economic slavery of humanity, and evil fomenting of continuous wars. This black magic of the Sun-Demon Sorat is neutralized by utilizing the Sun-forces of the Archai Michael, who is the current Time Spirit of our age since 1879, to directly confront this evil and dissolve it through faith, hope, wisdom, and love. The Archai Michael, who bears the countenance of Christ, helps conquer Sorat in our soul and spirit by working directly with the cosmic forces of Christ and his faithful Spirits of Form (Elohim) to battle Ahriman and the evil of the Anti-Christ Sorat, both of whom are fallen Spirits of Form. Through the mercy, grace, and love of Christ and His spiritual hierarchy, we can vanquish Sorat and his Asuras completely.

Michaelic souls will begin to perceive that the human etheric body is beginning to loosen from the physical, which creates the ability for focused thought to find a path to living imaginations. This loosening of the etheric body from the physical body is part of the mechanism for progressive human spiritual development. It is accompanied by the event of crossing the threshold between the physical and spiritual worlds.

Christ, Michael, and Sophia stand at the threshold to the spiritual world to protect and bear witness for the soul as it crosses the bridge between worlds. This same phenomenon is happening for humanity worldwide. As each person crosses the threshold, they learn that Christ guards the bridge as the Lord of Karma who weighs the soul each night. The Archai Michael and Sophia, who is the collective representative of the Spirits of Wisdom (Kyriotetes), help each person in the battle with evil as they wake-up in the morning and confront evil in the world. Christ is there as we fall asleep to be our karmic guardian and guide while Michael and Sophia are our special helpers upon crossing back across the threshold into the bright light of day.

Rudolf Steiner's Cosmology

In the West, a comprehensive and applicable cosmology can offer an antidote to Ahriman's incarnation and provide protection against the insatiable attacks of Ahriman, Lucifer, and the Asuras through Earth-bound materialism and the assault of hyper-technology. As the East tries to rectify issues concerning birth and overpopulation, the West wrestles with forces of death and ahrimanic enslavement to the unconscious use of technology that targets the destruction of the human ego. The healing forces of Central Europe provide the balance between East and West. The dynamic polarity between East and West creates a living spectrum of human challenges in the Earthly realm and the forces of healing from the Center help develop equanimity. The comprehension of the wisdom of karma and the understanding of reincarnation help build the bridge between East and West in a healing fashion. The wisdom of karma works through eugenic occultism and the knowledge of reincarnation works through mechanical occultism to heal the polarity between Lucifer and Ahriman. Both extremes are healed through love as the balancing mechanism between wisdom and the freedom—Christ between Lucifer and Ahriman. A full understanding of karma and reincarnation helps dispel the attacks of Lucifer and Ahriman.

Ahriman works through mathematical-mechanistic illusions of the world and through everything that divides people into small groups, nations, or narrow-minded interpretations of the Christian gospels. Ahriman will establish a great occult school which will make people magically into seers, but only confusion will reign from the many different versions of the spirit that these seers will describe. Constant strife will follow these differing views of the spirit. Many will claim the incarnation of Ahriman to be another incarnation of the Christ. Even though Christ came only once in a physical body and will not return again in the flesh, Ahriman will claim to be the second coming of Christ in a bodily fashion in place of the real cosmic Christ who now appears resurrected in the etheric realm. Ahriman will try to take the place of Christ entirely. He will attempt to become "immortal" in a human physical body augmented by mechanical occultism to try to defeat the mysteries of death that are so prevalent in the West. Ahriman will be blind to the living forces of Christ that are active in the etheric realm which are the renewing energies of immortal life. Both Lucifer and Ahriman are completely blind to the being of Christ and His forces that are active in creation.

Evil has its day, and then it must rest for a season. Evil in any form whether Lucifer, Ahriman, Sorat working through the Asuras, or the other beings who have fought against the evolution of human consciousness are owed a debt of gratitude for their sacrifices. Finding the middle path, the progressive evolution of Sophia Christos, defines the principal position of free will in human development that has been made possible by the evil forces of resistance. Human free will is not possible without the choice of the Tree of Good and Evil.

Evil wishes to steal human freedom through ahrimanic lies, luciferic temptations, and the machinations of the Asuras. The Great War in Heaven has come to Earth and each human soul is part of the battleground. Each perception, each thought, each feeling, each deed is an opportunity for love to be born out of a free deed, the most precious human creation. Every time an aspirant chooses a heavenly virtue instead of a deadly vice—evil is conquered like a dragon and tamed into a mighty force for good. In time, both the fallen Angel Lucifer and the dragon Ahriman can be used for good. This is the challenge of the aspirant who wishes to be become an initiate.

Since the turn of the millennium, humanity has been pulled across the threshold between the physical and spiritual worlds. This has separated the soul capacities of thinking, feeling and willing into independent agents uncontrolled by the human ego (I Am). This necessitates that the aspirant must directly meet and conquer Lucifer in his astral body through the capacity of moral thinking; conquer Ahriman in his etheric body through the capacity of moral feeling; and conquer the Asuras in his physical body through the capacity of moral willpower. Three battles are being waged for the soul of the human being and the aspirant must find Sophia (Wisdom) and Christ (Love) in both the physical and spiritual worlds as protectors while the soul is torn into three parts. Sophia Christos brings together the trinity of the soul into a unity of the spirit through the spiritual ego (I Am). The positive aspect of this battle is that the spiritual world stands ever closer to the human realm and is offering help to those who awaken and accept this help. Our guardian Angel wishes to help rid the soul of fear, doubt, and hatred if we would only accept the offer. The Holy Spirit and Sophia (AnthropoSophia) help midwife the process of crossing the threshold consciously to retain the cohesive control of thinking, feeling, and willing. The entire host of hierarchies stand ready to reveal the levels of consciousness beyond the human level to the anxious seeking soul, so that it might maintain cohesion of the soul in the spiritual world.

Understanding and taming Lucifer, Ahriman, and the Asuras is similar to the task of mastering the workings of the astral, etheric, and physical bodies. Taming Sorat is equivalent to saving your ego (I Am) from falling into the Eighth Sphere and developing your soul into its three higher spiritual principles of Spirit Self, Life Spirit, and Spirit Human (Angel, Archangel, Archai). It is also equal to the transformation of the soul capacities of thinking, feeling and willing into the higher spiritual capacities of Moral Imagination, Moral Inspiration, and Moral Intuition. The "three-headed dog of hell" (Lucifer, Ahriman, and Sorat) arises went the unprepared and unrepentant soul tries to enter the spiritual world without being morally prepared. To face this hound of hell, we need to remember that fear is conquered by faith, doubt by wisdom, and hatred by love. With these three virtues, Lucifer, Ahriman and the Asuras can be kept at bay, but it is the understanding of the Cosmic Christ, the Sophia of Christ, that is the force that cannot only control evil, but also transforms it into good. These are the healing forces of the Christ "Center" that balance the gifts and challenges of East and West. Christ's Love and Wisdom (Sophia) transform evil over time and redeem the efforts of Lucifer, Ahriman, and the Asuras into gifts for the Holy Spirit, the Father God, and Christ.

The Etheric Christ vs Ahrimanic Anti-Christ

Rudolf Steiner told us that, "Anthroposophy must develop as an entirely new seed within us, retaining from the dying part of mankind only what is cosmic, universal. Through Christ's death, quite new forces of life streamed out." (GA 310)

Dr. Steiner indicated in *The Reappearance of Christ in the Etheric,* Lecture I: *The Event of the Appearance of Christ in the Etheric World,* that the Etheric Christ would be able to be seen especially in 1933, 1935, and 1937. At that time, clairvoyant capacities will become natural abilities. Great changes will take place then and "Biblical prophecies will be fulfilled." Human souls will begin to develop "new faculties out of themselves", to exhibit "clairvoyant powers." He said that "a new age is at hand, in which the souls of human beings must take a step upward into the kingdom of heaven." Then, Christ will reappear because human beings will be raising themselves toward Him in the etheric realm.

Spiritual science is preparation for the return of Christ. Just as St. Paul, others will be "convinced through experiences in the etheric realm that Christ truly lives." Steiner said that the "greatest mystery of our time is the second coming of Christ." Human beings must advance to this "etheric vision" and perceive it in their own etheric body. Steiner speaks of the second coming of Christ and tells us that we must "raise ourselves up to Christ in the spiritual world by acquiring etheric vision." If humanity were to ignore the second coming of Christ in the etheric, the "vision of Christ in the etheric body would be limited to those who, through esoteric training, prove themselves to be ready to rise to such an experience."

In Lecture II of the book, *Spiritual Science as Preparation for a New Etheric Vision*, Steiner indicates that Paul was convinced Jesus was Christ when he "saw Christ clairvoyantly in the atmosphere of the Earth." Paul became convinced that the descent of Christ to the Earth consummated the ancient mysteries. Paul's experience of Christ in the atmosphere of the Earth can be clairvoyantly experienced after esoteric schooling or through natural clairvoyance that will become "entirely natural to humanity." This "Damascus Event" will be experienced by many people after 1933 as a return of Christ, where He is present for all those who are able to ascend as far as the "vision of the etheric body." Because Christ is always present within the etheric atmosphere of the Earth, the second coming of Christ will happen when human beings advance to "beholding Christ in the etheric."

In Lecture V of the book: *The Reappearance of Christ in the Etheric*, Steiner indicates that initiates in the past always went to "an ancient country" to "fetch from it" the guiding impulses of humanity and the "strength and wisdom for their missions." This land is often referred to as Shambhala or the fountainhead of the super-etheric realm, and ancient clairvoyants could see into these worlds like some sort of living fairyland. Shambhala is said to have risen into the atmosphere and become invisible. Shambhala will be seen again, at first only for a few, then for more and more human beings. This wisdom-woven, light-gleaming Shambhala abounds in infinite fullness of life that fills hearts with wisdom. Christ is the Lord of this etheric realm of Shambhala, also called the realm of Spiritual Economy.

It is from this realm that understanding of the cosmic nature of the deed of Christ flows forth as wisdom. The more humans can witness Christ in this realm, the more they will be able to understand the wisdom in the Gospels. As we grow into this mysterious land of Shambhala, it is possible to have a Damascus Event wherein the aspirant directly encounters the living Christ in the etheric realm, just as Paul did on the road to Damascus. The initiate rises into this land and experiences a kind of etheric revelation or apocalypse, an uncovering of the soul. This experience can be the foundation for a "new faith" or "religion of one." A direct dialogue begins with the being of Christ as He appears as a "second coming" for the awakened initiate.

Christ only comes to Earth once in a physical body; He now appears in His etheric body to awakened souls as a natural initiation. According to the level of the initiate, a spiritual kingdom can be felt surrounding him that is led by Christ who will be acknowledged by all who rise into the etheric realm, no matter what prior religious affiliations. Clear waking consciousness is the tool to enter this land under the guidance of Christ. The initiate must go there often to draw new forces from the radiant light and enter the portal to the land of the super-etheric Shambhala.

In *The Return of Christ*, Steiner goes further to say that new faculties will arise in humanity that will be able to perceive the human etheric body. Another capacity will develop wherein the aspirant will be able to look within himself and behold a dream-like picture that is the karmic outcome of a deed about to be performed. This is a prefiguring or precognitive perception, but not a dream. It is a "seeing into the karma of a deed," which gives us an awakening of responsibility for the karmic outcome of an action.

Eventually, all of the faculties attained by initiation will become universal faculties of humanity. Human beings with etheric clairvoyance will behold the Christ appearing before them in an etheric body. This etheric vision is a spiritual seed in the soul that awaits development by the individual. More and more, over time, humanity will develop the capacities to see Christ appearing in the etheric realm and grow so close to Him that they feel they can obtain consolation and strength directly from Him. They will receive instruction from Him and will know the right choices to make in life that align with morality, love, and wisdom. Each new instruction is like another letter in the alphabet that constructs a "language of the spirit." A true and living cosmology provide the Moral Imaginations that are the foundation for the Language of the Spirit that instructs through morality. Only eternal truths are spoken in this language.

The more Moral Imagination and Moral Inspiration arise in the soul, the more the etheric Christ appears to the seeker as a universal cosmic being manifesting in the super-etheric realm around the Earth. Christ will appear to many more as time goes on and He will become the constant companion of those who can attune to His presence, those who can raise their vibration to His etheric sphere.

In the past, Christ conquered what the human being experienced inwardly as the mystery of death. Christ conquered death and rose from the dead after three days to demonstrate that all humans are immortal and live on beyond death. Christ is now conquering what the human being experiences as the mystery of evil. He has already conquered Lucifer and turned his deeds to service in the evolution of humanity. Currently, Christ is battling with and conquering the forces of Ahriman. Lucifer lends a hand whenever Ahriman's deceptions win over another soul to materialism. The Asuras work with Ahriman and hope that the Sun Demon himself will come to Earth to rule as the ultimate Anti-Christ. These battles and forces are waging in the soul of every human being. When a battle is won, Christ shines forth over the forces of evil and reminds the soul that He has already conquered death and given immortality as a gift to every awakened soul. Christ now needs our help to conquer the cold, dark forces of Ahriman and the ego consuming forces of Sorat.

The Seventh Epoch

After the Seventh Age of Civilization, the War of All against All will break out [again] in a most terrible way. Great and mighty evil forces will be let loose by new technological discoveries, turning the whole Earth-globe into a kind of self-functioning, living electric mass like a spider web encircling the Earth. During this seventh age, cleverness without morality will be non-existent and only wisdom will effectively guide the soul. Christ will appear in a heavenly cosmic ego that evolves into a collective Christened Group-Soul of Humanity. Then, in a way that cannot be discussed, a tiny handful will be protected and preserved and carried forward into the next age.

In the Sixth Epoch, humans will witness the descending astral world, which is to say the images, expressions, and manifestations of human desire. The Seventh Epoch will bring about the descending of the heavenly world (Shambhala or New Jerusalem). After that, the Earth will have reached the goal of its physical evolution and together with all its beings will evolve into an astral heavenly body. Most physical substance, as such, will disappear. The part which until then had been able to spiritualize itself, will pass over into the spirit, into astral substance.

Imagine that all the beings of the Earth who up to that time have been able to express what is good, noble, and beautiful in their external material form will bear an expression of Christ Jesus in their countenance. Their words will manifest Christ Jesus, for they will ring out as living, resounding thoughts. These beings, through their spiritual efforts, are now preparing for their spiritual evolution and ascension and will eventually have the power to dissolve what they have within them as physical matter, just as warm water dissolves salt. Everything physical will pass over into an astral globe. Those who up to that time have not progressed so far as to be material and corporeal expressions of what is true, beautiful, and good will not have the power to dissolve matter; for them matter will remain. They will become hardened in matter, and being unable to dissolve their material form they will remain on in the physical world as slug-like beings during the Future Jupiter incarnation of the Earth, in the Eighth Sphere. In this way, Earth will advance towards its future.

Through the souls gradually refining matter from within, the substance of the Earth will become more and more refined until it receives the power to dissolve. Then will come the time when the insoluble part will be ejected as a slag Moon.

In the course of seven planetary incarnations, that which has hardened itself in matter will be driven out and the power which drives it out will be the opposite force to that which will have forced the good beings upward.

Beings become capable of dissolving matter through taking love into their souls. The more the soul is warmed by Christ's love, the more powerfully will it be able to work on matter; it will spiritualize the whole Earth and transform it into an astral globe. But just as love dissolves matter like warm water dissolves salt, so will the opposite of love press down everything which has not become capable of fulfilling the Earth mission. Just as during the fourth age of civilization love was imprinted in humanity, it will later become warmer and warmer through the last stages in our epoch, the sixth and seventh. On the other hand, that which continues to harden and solidify in matter will encounter divine wrath and be "left behind" with cold physical matter.

In the Seventh Epoch, the sounding of the trumpets will be heard, and the initiate will see with spiritual vision how ascended humans consist of delicate, spiritualized bodies rising up from the physical Earth; they will also see those who have hardened into materialism and how they are left behind on the surface of the Earth which will be deposited in the slag moon of the Eighth Sphere during Future Jupiter.

The Distant Future

The advantage of a comprehensive cosmology, as provided by Rudolf Steiner, is that the entire past and future are spelled out in specific terms. Amazing images of the far distant past and unimaginable predictions about humanity's future are part of the overall picture that depict humans as thinking, free beings who eventually become Angels, Archangels, and Archai. This sweeping panorama of Steiner's spiritual scientific view of the past and the future is breath-taking and sublime. It places the human being as an integral and critical player in the evolution of history, both physically and spiritually. The nature of the future human being is predicted to be Angelic, not just a material evolution of ahrimanic humans derived from apes. In Steiner's cosmology, virtue wins the battle against vices and all beings are reunited with the source and fountain of creation. There is no room for pessimism and nihilism when each human being should be busy learning the language of Angels so that he may consciously undertake his own spiritual development. The goal and intent of creation is the foundation of a worldview, a cosmology. If a spiritual cosmology fills the mind of an aspirant, then it is spirit that the seeker will find. Cosmology is the roadmap to our future nature and the picture of who we shall become.

In this abbreviated "Biography of Ahriman", it is hoped that the reader has useful images and descriptions of Ahriman and Lucifer and sees how their roles play out in one's personal life. They aren't imaginary beings that exist in a realm of fantasy; they are close and personal in our souls and have actual human incarnations in history. We need to absorb the ancient wisdom that Lucifer brought to the East and glean the usefulness of Ahriman's incarnation in our own time. Balance is the source of mastering Lucifer and Ahriman through the loving heart forces of Christ filled with the wisdom of Sophia (Anthroposophia). It is this middle way that leads us and other members of the "School of Michael" to confront and conquer the forces of the dragon in our time. Steiner is the great prophet and seer of the Michaelic Age and has pointed us in the direction where our personal growth and development unfold in a healthy fashion. We are gods in the making according to Steiner, and our challenge is that as we become more "divine", the more we must face the darkness of evil and need to muster the forces to bring light, love, and wisdom as the antidote.

We should not be overwhelmed with the knowledge of evil in our time. The stronger these forces of resistance grow, the stronger we will grow in our spiritual faith to overcome them. It is a challenge of our time to leave fear, doubt, and hatred behind and take on the cloaks of mercy, love, faith, and wisdom. These divine virtues can bind and conquer the forces of evil that will then become new capacities of soul and spirit developing into super-sensible organs of perception with the ability to understand that all evil shall one day be redeemed. The grand perspective of a complete cosmology gives the aspirant a vantage point of clarity and breadth of perception that places everything in its rightful position. Everything in the Cosmos has its place, time, and reason for being and a comprehensive cosmology provides that assurance. When we find out the true nature of each of these beings, we will find that they have come to help us and advance our spiritual evolution.

Rudolf Steiner's Anthroposophy goes further back and further forward in time than any other spiritual teaching. To know the past and future is a rare gift, and we have through Steiner a singular teaching that has made hundreds of prophecies about human destiny, many of which have already come to pass just as he predicted. Steiner's prophecies of the future are easier to handle when we know that so much of his indications have come to pass just as he prophesized. This gives the cosmology of Steiner more weight than others, and more utility for advancing spiritual development. We are fortunate in that we can count on the predictions of Steiner to continue to come true, especially in relationship to the developing human being.

It is often pointless to project too far into the future because most people are not prepared for what is to come and can barely handle the challenges of the present. Studying Steiner's teachings is a key to building the capacities of higher thought (Moral Imagination) that is necessary to envision the far distant future. According to Steiner, our current Moon will eventually break apart and reunite with Earth. The Earth itself will then break apart and become a globe that is left behind by those who rise to meet the super-human beings descending from the future Earth incarnations of Future Jupiter, Future Venus, and Future Vulcan— the superhumans from Venus, Mercury, and Vulcan. During the Future Jupiter incarnation of the Earth, there will be two Moons, one being the Eighth Sphere and another inhabited by black magicians. The humans that do not keep up with the evolution of the progressive spirits will find themselves on the surface of the old Earth in terrible conditions or in the Eighth Sphere. Progressive humans, who now have evolved into Angels, will try to help these "animal-humans" attempt to evolve. Angel-humans will become the guardian Angels of these animal-humans who choose to remain behind. The progressive spirits will live in communities that are like spiritual spheres that float in the atmosphere above the old Earth, and the two Moons, while drinking in their nourishment directly from the Sun.

During the Future Venus and Future Vulcan incarnations of Earth, we, as progressive spirits, will learn to communicate more and more with higher hierarchical beings as we become more like them as we develop further the Language of the Spirit and understand the workings of the Divine Plan. All material substance will be left behind in those incarnations of the Earth and our non-material planet of Future Venus will begin to merge with the Sun. We will eventually become spirits of the Sun and will join with the beings that already live on the Sun. We will become Christened beings through this wedding with the Solar Logos of Christ and will become part of the Christened Group-Soul of Humanity.

When the progressive spirits finally reach their own Christened selves, they can evolve even beyond that stage to the condition of becoming what Steiner calls, a Zodiac. Each one of us may become a Zodiac, a Cosmos unto ourselves. These thoughts are far beyond human comprehension at this point in evolution and cannot truly be imagined properly. They are beyond the levels of developed Moral Imagination and Moral Inspiration. To have human knowledge of these future stages requires direct Moral Intuition to experience them. They are truly mysteries of the future that require our third and highest Ego (Spirit Human) to experience. These are the mysteries of evolution implicit in Steiner's Anthroposophical cosmology that can a blessing in our times.

The Future of Machines

The Karma of Vocation, Rudolf Steiner, Dornach, April 27, 1916, GA 172

"A time will come when a machine will stand there motionless, at rest, and a man will step up to it who knows that he has to make a certain movement with his hand, then another movement in a particular way, and then a third, and through the air-vibrations produced by this definite signal, the motor, having been tuned to this signal, will be set in motion.

In steam engines, ahrimanic demons are brought right down to the point of physical incorporation. This means that while the Cosmos with its spiritual element has descended through what has been poured into human evolution, the spirituality of the Cosmos is driven out through what is created in the form of demons. This great and wonderful modern progress has in fact brought about not only a demonology, but a demon magic; and in manifold ways modern technology is demon magic. Here you can see quite directly how vibrations are given over to the demon, so that he can develop his activity outwards into cosmic space.

Wherever electricity and much else is used, there is far more demon magic, for electricity operates with quite different forces which have a different significance for the Cosmos. Anyone who understands Spiritual Science will naturally know clearly that these things are not to be done away with; that we cannot be reactionary or conservative in the sense of opposing progress. Indeed, demon magic signifies progress, and the Earth will make more and more progress of this kind. A stage will even be reached when it will be possible to produce great effects outwards into the Cosmos.

Humanity must learn to deal with nature as the gods themselves have done, not building machines in an indifferent way, but doing everything as an act of divine service and bringing the sacramental into everything."

Ahrimanic Sub-Nature

The Michael Mystery, From Nature to Sub-Nature, Rudolf Steiner, Chapter XXIX, GA 26

"By far the greater part of all that is at work through the agency of technical science in the civilization of today is not Nature, but Sub-Nature. It is a world which is emancipating itself from Nature, downwards. And as he penetrates into this merely Earthly realm, he encounters the world of Ahriman. He must learn to bring himself and his own human being into right relation with this ahrimanic element.

As yet, in the course hitherto taken by the Technical Age, he has not found the way to readjust his human relation rightly to this new civilization of Ahriman. Man must find the strength, the inner faculty of knowledge and discernment, for his human being not to be overwhelmed by Ahriman in the civilization of technology. Sub-Nature must be understood in this, its character of being "under" Nature. It will only be so understood if man rises at least as high in spiritual knowledge of that Super-Nature, which lies outside the Earthly sphere, as he has descended in technical science below it into Sub-Nature.

Electricity must be recognized in its own peculiar power to lead down from Nature to Sub-Nature. But man must not glide down with it.

In a Science of the Spirit the other sphere is created, from which an ahrimanic element is altogether absent. It is precisely by taking into his mind that form of spiritual intelligence to which the ahrimanic Powers have no access, that man gains the strength to meet Ahriman in the world, to encounter him here."

The Battle Between Humans and Machines

The following article was first written on our neoanthroposophy.com website as a warning to readers that we are in a war between human intelligence and machine intelligence. This war has already had many casualties through illnesses connected to electromagnetic sensitivity, digital addiction, cyber-bullying, anti-social disassociation, and numerous other technology disorders that are plaguing our high-tech age. The article is published in its original format.

We are engaged in a raging battle to defend the living etheric realm from the forces of darkness that intend to crucify Christ again and prevent His "Second Coming" in the etheric realm of the Earth, Cosmos, and human etheric body. If you are not aware of this battle, then you may have already been overcome by the illusory and selfish cold light of Lucifer working in your astral body to make you feel like the king or queen of your own sub-natural realm of personal astral desires. Or perhaps the dead, grey light of Ahriman's delusion has already entered you and hypnotized you until your heart has become cold and devoid of selfless love. Many have been lulled into a lazy, comfortable surrendering of their will to the Asuras, who are inspired by Sorat the Sun Demon. Sorat intends to consume the human "I Am", in contradistinction to Christ's mission of re-enlivening the living etheric realm with His own cosmic etheric body that brings the waters of life and the grace of love to all who can arise to this realm and witness Christ's Second Coming in the etheric body of the Earth and humanity.

Rudolf Steiner tells us that the Second Coming of Christ in the etheric realm is the second most important focal point in human spiritual history. The Mystery of Golgotha, which is the life, death, and resurrection of Jesus Christ, is the most important turning point in human history. We are living in a crucial time for the development of humanity and each individual is a battleground in the spiritual war raging over human thinking, feeling, and willing. The outcome of this battle is not yet known, and the soul and spirit of each human can evolve into Super-Nature and develop higher thinking, feeling, and willing into the spiritual capacities of

Moral Imagination, Moral Inspiration, and Moral Intuition. These are higher realms governed and populated by Angels, Archangels, and Archai that work to help humans spiritually evolve.

On the other hand, the spiritual war for the etheric realm and the battle to stop the re-crucifixion of Christ can be lost and the soul and spirit of humanity be drawn into an evil realm of fallen spirits called the Eighth Sphere. This binary realm of two-dimensional beings is alluring, transfixing, and hypnotizing humanity into a Sub-Nature realm ruled by the condensing forces of electricity, the binding forces of electromagnetism, and the destructive and fragmenting forces of atom-based materialism intent on enslaving humanity in the Eighth Sphere. Only the forces of Christ can conquer the onslaught of Lucifer, Ahriman, and Sorat's Asuras.

To compound the battle, the physical being of Ahriman has already incarnated in North America as a counter-pole to the incarnation of Lucifer in Central Asia in the Third Millennium BC. Ahriman's influence is quite profound, and his materialistic, abstract, mathematical worldview has turned human thinking into machine-intelligence, a foreign and alien intelligence that is the "grey shadow-thinking" that Steiner describes that runs along the spider-web of electromagnetic lines encircling the Earth.

Human thinking, which can be filled with warmth and light when focused on virtue, love, and morality, is being turned into shadow images of cold light that draw the soul into dark selfishness. It is the Archai Michael's cosmic thoughts that should be drawing humans up into the realm of the etheric where higher, living thinking can become aligned with Angelic thinking in the manifestation of Moral Imagination. Instead, the unwitting warrior in this battle is pulled into his electrical device or digital virtual reality and soon begins thinking evil thoughts unconsciously as he gives his thoughts, feelings, and willpower over to the demon in the machine. The human double grows strong when it assumes it is personally deserving of the marvelous inventions that scientific materialism has placed at its disposal. This is tantamount to digital possession by evil beings who bring psychological, neurological, and sociological illnesses along with them.

Mechanical Omnipresence is a Delusion of the Heart

Consciousness and gratefulness are keys to overcoming the immense technological forces that wish to draw from the human being its future spiritual development and replace it with hedonistic, selfish, immediate gratification that makes the user of the device a thief in the night who takes advantage of other people's computer programming and effort without gratitude or consciousness. The modern technology user is given what seems to be super-human powers in the palm of her hand. The user can ask any question of her device and have the answer almost instantaneously via a search of the Internet, where almost all knowledge is stored and easily accessed. Any question can be answered by the user's seemingly omniscience electromagnetic computer-driven device. Almost anything that has ever been written down, or any video that has ever been filmed, or any data byte of knowledge ever recorded, can be available to the uninformed, uneducated, and generally ignorant tech-user who can now look like a "god of knowledge" via the Ahrimanic device. This Luciferic temptation of "knowing all" is an illusion and lures the users into ever growing unconsciousness as grey shadow-thinking, that is found in the virtual world of machine-intelligence, takes over human-intelligence.

The tech-user learns from an alien-intelligence (AI) and then pridefully believes that they are smarter than other humans and have even become a superior thinker. The spiritual scientist, on the other hand, becomes a thinker who has warmed his thoughts with love, instead of a selfish ego-illusion of superiority developed through materialistic thinking. This astral illusion, created by Lucifer, draws thinking into the trap of enslavement in a personal world of seeming technological omniscience.

When a user of tech-science becomes fluent in social media on the Internet, they can reach all their contacts instantaneously, no matter how far away they live. The tech-user's social media account may have thousands of friends, and they may participate in hundreds of groups. When they send out a message, it may reach millions of people instantly, and if they post an interesting video or URL link, they may get millions of "hits" and "likes." The more hits, the more stimulating the mechanical interaction can be, which may engender an addiction to the process of tech-stimulation. Internet addiction is a well-known disorder in the modern age. This type of delusion, believing you are communicating with many others, is seemingly a type of technological omnipresence. The idea that you can be everywhere at one time is magical thinking, and yet machines convince us that we have friends we have never met in person. The tech-user has traveled all over the world through Flicker, Google Earth, or live-feeds of video cameras all over the world that make the users think they are truly global citizens. Mechanical Omnipresence is a delusion of the heart that fosters a tech-user's belief that they are a social person and a well-liked individual, even though they may speak "in person" with no one.

Tech-science has created a form of omnipotence through the software and hardware called, The Internet of Things. This program controls your entire life from your phone and coordinates your personal life, work life, and global life through one system that links every digital device you own to one central command system. Net-bots link your doorbell, microwave, house lights, alarms, coffeemaker, car, computers, and everything else to your smart-phone. You can program your net-bots to react as soon as your phone passes by and it can create an augmented reality to the real world that essentially steals your willpower unconsciously.

Your entire life can be programmed into the Internet of Things, until the line between human and machine blurs. If you have a house in a distant place and want to turn on the sprinkler system because your phone informs you it has been quite hot there, you simply push a button, and the Internet of Things seems to be omnipotent and can reach out and effect net-bots anywhere on the planet. This omnipotence is not earned or deserved by the tech-user and tends to lure, hypnotize, and imprison the unconscious and unwitting user in an anti-human virtual world.

The spiritual scientist knows that omniscience, omnipresence, and omnipotence are products of the future spiritual development of humanity. In time, as we become Angels, Archangels, and Archai we will develop higher thinking, feeling, and willing that resembles these stages of consciousness. Lucifer, Ahriman, and the Asuras inspired by Sorat, try to bring these future stages of spiritual development to humanity through mechanical means—a type of mechanical clairvoyance, clairaudience, and clairsentience—mechanical occultism.

Ahriman himself will start a "school of spiritual clairvoyance" that will delude followers into believing that they are becoming clairvoyant through mechanical means. Ahrimanic clairvoyants will not agree on what they "see" because they will be looking at grey shadow-thoughts of the spiritual world which will be tinged with the base astral nature of the person and thus will produce spurious results which lead to spiritual materialism and ultimately spiritual devolution.

Lucifer's enticing allure, Ahriman's brilliant cleverness, and the overwhelming power of the Asuras to consume the human ego are the weapons we must fight against in the battle in the etheric realm to guarantee the etheric resurrection of Christ and assure His second coming. We must become conscious of this battle between good and evil and find our personal place in this cosmic war.

The great cosmic battle is within our very own etheric body, and we cannot escape it. The war is also collective and takes place in the etheric sheaths around the Earth that Rudolf Steiner called: the realm of spiritual economy, the etheric ring, Shamballa, the New Jerusalem, and the living realm of Angelic Moral Imagination. Without the good health of the Earth's etheric sheaths, the human etheric body cannot be healthy.

The Battle Rages All Around You

The battle for the soul is within us, but it is also waged outside of us in the etheric body of Mother Earth, the realm of the Spirits of Wisdom, the Beings of the Kyriotetes. The personal battle for our own life-body affects every person on the Earth, as well as the future life of our planet. If we lose the battle individually, we will reside in the Eighth Sphere after death in a physical two-dimensional world instead of evolving through time into the fourth dimension and beyond, where the higher hierarchies dwell.

The battle is raging, and the losers are quietly ignoring the enemy's most deadly weapons, which are clasped in their own hands. They don't realize that weaponized subliminal programming is coming from every digital device and that they swim in a continuum of electromagnetic frequencies that bombard them from all directions with poisonous electromagnetic broadcast frequencies. Sorat's digital weapons have lulled the innocent user into believing they are virtual kings and queens in their own selfish domain. When fallen Angels stand ready to do the tech-user's bidding, it is hard to lay down the harmful weapons that have come to define who we believe we are in this modern, materialistic world of technology.

One large solar flare could wipe out all digital memory and electromagnetism on the Earth for a long period of time. The losers in this battle would simply stop existing as the being they thought they were when they were augmented with miraculous digital machines that were the weapons of their enemies. The Internet is out of control and at this point controls commerce, education, and social life in the West. The modern teenager might "die" if all of Ahriman's weapons ceased to function. Thus, it is easy to see the true control Sorat and his followers have over the "I Am" of the human being ensnared as a tech-user.

- Are there solutions to the war in heaven that have now come down to Earth?
- Are there spiritual scientific weapons that can be used against the enemy as Michael used the sword of God to strike Lucifer down from heaven?
- Can we consciously face the evils of Lucifer, Ahriman, Sorat, the Asuras, and scientific materialism and win the battle?
- Where do we look for assistance in this battle and find a way through that doesn't just simply reject all technology?
- Did Rudolf Steiner show us a path through the mechanical take-over of human evolution?
- Should we ignore or combat the incarnation of Ahriman?
- What can protect us in this war for the soul and spirit of each human being?

The answer to these questions is simple: With Michael's sword of the spirit, and the Word of God, we can win the war against evil.

One of the best descriptions of the spiritual weapons that can protect and defend us during this war is found in the *Bible, in Ephesians 6:12-17*:

> "For we wrestle not against flesh and blood, but against principalities, against powers, against the rulers of the darkness of this world, against spiritual wickedness in high places. Wherefore take unto you the whole armor of God, that ye may be able to withstand in the evil day, and having done all, to stand. Stand therefore, having your loins girt about with truth, and having on the breastplate of righteousness; and your feet shod with the preparation of the gospel of peace; above all, taking the shield of faith, wherewith ye shall be able to quench all the fiery darts of the wicked. And take the helmet of salvation, and the sword of the Spirit, which is the Word of God…"

With the armor of God, truth, righteousness, peace, faith, salvation, the sword of the Spirit, and the Word of God, we can win the battle and gain victory in the war against the "principalities, powers, darkness of the world, and spiritual wickedness in high places", according to the author of *Ephesians*. These spiritual weapons may seem tame compared to the "spiritual wickedness in high places" but they hold the key to divesting evil's power.

The "higher" beings of evil that are described, are actually fallen hierarchy who are far more advanced than human consciousness at this point in human spiritual development. We are fighting beings of the rank of hierarchies called Spirits of Form. Sorat was a Spirit of Form who fell from grace. Ahriman and Lucifer have fallen also, and they are from the higher realms of the "principalities", "powers", and "high places" referred to in the quotation.

We need to know the names and the nature of the evil that we must confront to maintain proper spiritual evolution throughout this battle for the soul and spirit of humanity. We have heard about the "fallen" ones and their wicked natures that use evil methods for luring, entrancing, and hypnotizing tech-users. What we need to know now is how to antidote evil's intent and what spiritual beings are there to help us counter the evil war raging all around us.

Christ will defeat the evil intentions of Sorat and his ego-eating Asuras. Christ works through the combined forces of the Seven Elohim, who lead the Spirits of Form (Powers). Sorat, like Lucifer, consciously fell from grace and stood against the proper evolution of human development. Sorat wants to steal the egos that Christ helped create and plant in each human being. Christ gives to humans their personal egos until a higher ego can be developed out of wisdom, grace, and love.

Each personal, guardian Angel stands ready to help the evolving soul find their higher spirit. The Holy Spirit of Christ also works directly with the personal guardian Angel to imbue the individual with the gifts of "The Comforter" of Christ.

Another being who works in the realm of the human being's Angel is the being Rudolf Steiner calls AnthropoSophia. This being works intimately with each person who is questing for their higher self. In the past, AnthropoSophia has been called other names: TheoSophy, PhiloSophy, Isis Sophia, AnthropoSophia, and Sophia Christos—the Cosmic Wisdom of Christ. Steiner gives many details about our personal relationship with AnthropoSophia, who he calls the midwife of our spirit-birth. With the help of AnthropoSophia, the Holy Spirit can redeem the "selfish thoughts" of Lucifer and turn them into the unselfish cosmic thoughts of the Archai Michael, who is the leading Time Spirit (Archai) of our age. Through the Holy Spirit and AnthropoSophia, human thoughts can become imbued with the Spirits of Wisdom (Kyriotetes) and become Michaelic cosmic thoughts. This process is one antidote to Ahriman's grey shadow-thinking.

From the realm of the Archangels, Michael has ascended and progressed to the hierarchical rank of the Archai in 1879 AD, becoming the Spirit of the Times, our current Zeitgeist. After his regency, Michael will remain in the ranks of the Archai. The being known by the name Vidar, in Norse Myths, has progressed into an Archangelic position filling the rank previously held by the Archangel Michael. Vidar manifests in the human etheric body and works with Archangels to inspire humanity and lead it toward the spiritual realms. The Being of Wisdom, called Sophia, also works into the realm of the Archangels from the hierarchical rank of the Kyriotetes. The Beings of Wisdom are directly linked to the Archangels and their evolution during the Old Sun incarnation of the Earth, especially in relationship to the nature of thinking itself. Humans can turn to Vidar, Sophia, and the Archangels that guide human language and culture to assist in battling Ahriman's assault upon the human etheric body.

To help defeat the Asuras attack on the physical body, we can turn to the rank of the Archai for spiritual assistance. Michael is now the leader of this realm of Time Spirits and is engaged in defending all souls who can ascend to the realm of direct Moral Intuition and alignment with the divine. Michael does not "dip down" to fight and defend us. We must "rise-up" to his realm of wisdom-filled cosmic-thinking and truly engage our will in the battle for the etheric, the war to stop the second crucifixion of Christ in the etheric realm and bring forth the Second Coming of Christ.

Michael sounds the trumpet to awaken the spiritual scientists who must become warriors of wisdom, love, and strength. We must become victors of truth, beauty, and goodness to defeat selfishness, fear, doubt, and hatred. The spiritual warrior must find the strength and courage to develop higher consciousness that can banish evil from human spiritual self-development and bring forth the higher gifts and capacities of the Spirit Self, Life Spirit, and Spirit Human, the three spiritual components of the human being.

We are aided and helped from all sides in the war against evil that intends to steal the thinking, feeling, and willing of the human being and capture it in a binary, material world that vampirizes the life and spirit from humans. The evil beings of a higher nature working against us may seem too overwhelming to tackle, but when we remember all the other spiritual beings who are supporting and fighting along with us, we can muster the courage to pick up Michael's banner of Christ-Sophia and surge forward in the efforts to vanquish evil and gain our spiritual home and inheritance.

The Cosmic and Earthly Battle Rages On

There is a cosmic and earthly battle raging over whether universal thinking (Moral Imagination) will be lost to humanity for good. The decisive war in heaven has descended to the Earth in the year 1840 AD, because the Archai Michael cast both Lucifer and Ahriman (the dragon) to the Earth. Heaven has fallen to Earth, and the last battle for human freedom is being fought in the human domain. The Norse called this war in heaven, the Battle of Ragnarok wherein the "old gods" died, and the "young gods" live on to find a new home. In the West, we call it the Apocalypse. The apocalyptic "two-horned beast" is the new machine-realm of binary forces that are trying to steal the soul and spirit of humanity.

There are many terrifying images describing the horrors of the Apocalypse but there are also other images that show the healing antidotes to apocalyptic horror. In the end, those who can "hear and sing the new song" are saved as they gather around the Lion of Judah, who has tamed the "two-horned beast." Even the very methods to develop the counter-image of the "two-horned beast" are given in the Apocalypse, for "those with eyes to see and ears to hear."

Rudolf Steiner describes the battle between Michael and Ahriman/Sorat in the following characterization:

"The entry of Michael into the spiritual evolution of mankind at the end of the 19th century, and that of the etheric Christ in the first half of the 20th century, will be followed before the close of this century by the coming of the Sun-Demon. In our present Michaelic Age we have every reason, if we wish to work in the domain of theology, of religion, to turn above all to what the Apocalypse can teach us, to learn to think and feel apocalyptically, to raise ourselves up to the spiritual impulses working behind outer existence." (GA 346)

Rudolf Steiner refers to our apocalyptic times as a second crucifixion of Christ in the etheric realm, in the following indication:

"The seeds of Earthly materialism, which from the sixteenth century onward were brought into the spiritual world in ever greater measure by souls passing the portal of death, spread darkness there, producing the "black sphere" of materialism. In a Manichean way, Christ took this black sphere into His own being in order to transform it. But this caused the death by spiritual suffocation of the Angel-Being, through whom Christ had manifested Himself since the Mystery of Golgotha. This was Christ's sacrifice in the nineteenth century, a sacrifice comparable to that of His physical life in the Mystery of Golgotha. It can be regarded as a second crucifixion of Christ in the etheric realm." (GA 152)

The battle for the soul of humanity is being fought in the realm of the Time Spirits where Michael, the current Time Spirit and representative of Christ, is battling the Asuras who are inspired by the fallen Spirit of Form, Sorat the Sun Demon. This battle reaches all the way down into the human physical body and controls the fate of the human ego, or "I Am."

Rudolf Steiner speaks about Sorat the Sun Demon, in the following manner:

"Sorat is the being that draws the future into the present and the present into the past. Sorat seeks to sever man's connection with the divine-spiritual and pull him into its own dark sphere of evil. The time of thrice 666, 1998, now stands before us. At the end of this century, we shall reach the moment when Sorat will raise his head most powerfully above the flowing stream of evolution, when he will oppose that vision of Christ which human beings, who have prepared themselves for it, can have through the appearance of the etheric Christ in the first half of the 20th century. There are only two

thirds of a century left, before Sorat will emerge with great power."
(GA 346)

When we look at the man-machine interface, we can learn from Steiner's lecture on January 28, 1923, about the true nature of electricity:

> "The greatest contrast to electricity is light. If we look upon light as electricity, we confuse good and evil. When we think of them as atoms, in general, when we imagine matter in the form of atoms, we transform them into carriers of evil, carriers of death. For electric atoms are little demons of evil.
>
> Michael would find Cosmic Intelligence again at a time when an Intelligence intensely exposed to the ahrimanic forces and bereft of spirituality had taken root among men. For while the Intelligence was descending from the Cosmos to the Earth, the aspirations of the ahrimanic powers grew ever greater, striving to wrest the Cosmic Intelligence from Michael.
>
> Such was the crisis from the beginning of the 15th century until our day, which expresses itself as the battle of Ahriman and Michael. For Ahriman is using all his power to challenge Michael's dominion over the Intelligence that has now become earthly. And Michael, with all the impulses that are his, through his dominion over the intelligence has fallen from him, is striving to take hold of it again on Earth at the beginning of his new earthly rule. So, Michael finds himself obliged to defend against Ahriman what he had ruled through eons of time for the benefit of humankind. Mankind stands in the midst of this battle; and among other things, to be an anthroposophist is to understand this battle."

Ahriman is engaged in a battle to win the etheric body of the human being as he works through the realm of thinking to turn human-thought into machine-thought and numb humans to the power of living thinking that is fired by the warmth of the heart. The Archai Michael is involved in this battle and tames the "dragon of materialism" by bringing the cosmic wisdom and love of Sophia and Christ.

Lucifer is battling in the astral body of the human being through the realm of the Angels where the Holy Spirit and the being, AnthropoSophia, support the development of the Consciousness Soul evolving into the Spiritual Self.

Rudolf Steiner describes this cosmic battle in the following remarks:

"Ahriman stands before us as a cosmic being of the highest imaginable Intelligence, one who has already taken the Intelligence entirely into the individual, personal element. If ever we let ourselves in for a discussion with Ahriman, we should inevitably be shattered by the logical conclusiveness, the magnificent certainty of aim with which he manipulates his arguments. In Ahriman's opinion, the really decisive question is this: Will cleverness or stupidity prevail? And Ahriman calls stupidity everything that does not contain Intelligence within it in full personal individuality.

Michael, however, is not in the least concerned with the personal quality of Intelligence. We human beings are always tempted to make our Intelligence personal as Ahriman has done. But Michael will only administer the Cosmic Intelligence and not make it personally his own. And now that people have the Intelligence, it should again be administered by Michael as something belonging to all humanity—as the common and universal Intelligence that benefits all of us alike. Behind the scenes of existence is raging the battle of Michael against all that is of Ahriman. Michael is a spirit filled with strength, and he can only make use of brave people who are full of courage." (GA 236)

The Binary World of the Two-Horned Beast

The pseudo-alive kingdom of the machine-world that exists between the mineral and the plant realms wishes to feed on human thought, to steal it, and suck it into another world beyond the three-dimensional world. This world is called the Eighth Sphere by theosophists and is a leftover sphere from the seven incarnations of the Earth. The Eighth Sphere is now a machine-world that exists in an "anti" two-dimensional world. It is a shadow of the angelic realm which is made from mineral substance and given pseudo-life through the thoughts of the software programmers. It is an alien world populated by beings higher and lower than human beings, which exist both in this anti-two-dimensional world and in the binary world of electromagnetic beings. The software program routines and sub-routines that all work together to make our human-machine interfaces work well to create "energy efficient" and "labor saving" tools for human beings that ultimately steal human thinking by making us mentally lazy, freezing human feeling with cold, dead machine-intelligence and binary logic and paralyze the user who is fascinated, transfixed, and hypnotized by the "seeming miracle" of the machine.

Instead of evolving into the fourth dimension, humans are being lured back into a two-dimensional binary existence in the alien two-dimensional world of machine-intelligence. When we devolve into the past through the hypnotic entrancement of fascinating binary illusion, we give up our future progressive spiritual development. We give our own ego development over to beings who are not really in our 3D world and therefore are not "seen" as harmful forces—let alone an evil being. These stories make the frail-of-heart run away from technology, like a dragon that is trying to eat them. In fact, this is quite true on a soul and spiritual level of understanding. As the Asuras are stealing the will of the hypnotized user of the Internet, smartphone, or computer they suck the life-force of the user into a sphere of existence that is outside of the normal evolutionary seven spheres of Earth evolution. This sphere is referred to as the Eighth Sphere which is being built in a two-dimensional world that interpenetrates our world of three-dimensional world. When the human being can add to the third dimension the understanding of time—timelessness—then a fourth dimension can be added to the third dimension in the consciousness of the aspirant. Luciferic, Ahrimanic, or Asuric beings are able to steal the thinking, feeling, and willing of the human being through luring them into the binary world of the past where they add stolen human forces to the Eight Sphere. These evil beings attempt to lure the human soul into the fallen realm of the Eighth Sphere after death, instead of passing into higher spheres.

Being	Body	Realm	Soul Force	Sub-Nature	Super-Nature
Lucifer	Astral	Angels	Thinking	Electricity	Imagination
Ahriman	Etheric	Archangel	Feeling	Magnetism	Inspiration
Asuras/Sorat	Physical	Archai-Time	Willing	Third Force	Intuition

Rudolf Steiner speaks of Lucifer and Ahriman's victory in a most powerful way in this selection:

"Everything is going to be mechanized. Handwriting will go out of use; children will learn directly to type on typewriters. The future will be dominated by the mechanization of life. This began with the invention of the steam engine, and in future ages people will look back on the invention as Ahriman's victory, just as we look back on man's fall into original sin as Lucifer's victory. When the steam engine was introduced at the end of the eighteenth century, the Gods handed over to Ahriman the material evolution of the Earth. The remainder of Earth evolution with its machines and its mechanization belongs to Ahriman. The Gods have given it over into his hands. This is a fact which, like the explosion of a bomb, should shake us to the very depths of our souls." (GA 140)

Illusion of Lucifer, Delusion of Ahriman, Confusion of Asuras

The occult annihilation of the human soul happens in the realm of the Time Spirits where Michael has ascended to as the leading Archangel who has become an Archai. Sorat, the Sun Demon, is a laggard Being of Form (Elohim), acting in the realm of the Archai; therefore, is in direct confrontation with the Archai Michael. Michael is also a Sun being who is the "countenance of Christ" and his chosen defender who has been given a sword of power. Michael has already used that sword to cast Lucifer from "before the throne of God", down to the Earth. Michael also cast the "dragon" down from the heavens to the Earth with the sword of power.

Lucifer works in the realm of the Angels to mislead human thinking. Ahriman works in the realm of the Archangels to freeze human feelings, while the Asuras work in the realm of the Archai to control human willing. Sorat is the Anti-Christ, the Sun Demon, who works through Ahriman and the Asuras to destroy the human I, the ego consciousness donated by Christ from the realm of the Sun.

Human Intelligence Vs. Machine Intelligence

Artificial Intelligence needs to be controlled by human intelligence and not the other way around. Machine-language hardware and software should not rule our lives, and we need to fully understand the effects of the software that drives the harmful hardware. Software, collectively speaking, is the accumulated thoughts and work of all the human programmers that went into the base code of an overall program. In other words, part of the "Artificial Intelligence" being attributed to machines is the combined efforts of millions of computer programmers. To conflate these two aspects of supposed "AI" is to mischaracterize the true nature of the illusion, delusion, and hypnotic effects of machine intelligence upon human intelligence. In essence, the smartphone or computer embodies a machine-realm of automated binary thought-systems. This is a new binary realm of machine archetypes, a new type of "machine-animal" that exists somewhere between the human and animal kingdoms utilizing minerals that have seemingly become alive like a plant. When these concepts are not consciously part of the tech-users mind, they are indeed black magic devices that steals the human beings "I Am."

Rudolf Steiner predicts these machine-animals that possess intelligence in the following indication:

> "The cosmic forces that will be brought into operation from this side will give rise to remarkable machines, but only of a kind that will relieve men of labor because they will bear in themselves a certain power of intelligence. And a spiritual science that itself reaches out to the Cosmos will have to take care that all the great temptations emanating from these machine-animals created by man himself will exercise no harmful influence on humanity." (GA 178)

Computer-driven calculating and data processing are labor saving machine-intelligences, whereas the digital binary worlds of the "Internet of Things" and the "Internet of the Body" are truly an artificial, alien intelligence inside of a virtual realm that appears alive and self-organizing. A human being is not evolved enough, at this stage, to wield this machine intelligence which produces virtual, mechanical omniscience, omnipresence, and omnipotence that the combined efforts of millions of human programmers have created via the Internet and the pervasive electromagnetic environment around us.

Individuals lack the moral uprightness to handle the power of the collective work of humans who have created an "intelligence system" of rigid sequences of thoughts mimicked by magnetized registers in machines that have replaced human thinking. These binary, magnetized registers that are a type of anti-physical living mineral, comprise a "machine-world" that no human can enter or comprehend. No single human being is deserving of this immense power of focused human labor from millions of programmers who created rigid machine intelligences that produce wonders and fascinate the beholder. No programmer can "look at" the binary machine language of the computer and translate the nature of what the language spells out in its alien code. Even programmers can't read machine language. They must incorporate different programming languages that speak to other sub-programming languages that turn that code into a machine generated series of zeroes and ones before the "fake light, sound, and life" in the computer can then "talk to us" in our human language.

The binary world serves the double (doppelganger) of the human being and helps create an extra "electric double" around the physical body that allows Ahriman to take ever stronger hold of the human constitution. This is most pronounced in America because the principal mountain ranges align with the north-south poles of the magnetic Earth and create an extra electric sheath around the human body—an extra electric double.

Binary thinking is always a polarity, and in nature there are no simple polarities. Nature is a trinity of forces: life, death, and rebirth. She is a spectrum of expressions, a continuum of diversity manifesting in life, and she cannot be fully fathomed. Nothing is ever black and white in the real world; everything is comprised of a variety of dynamic colors and shades. Dialectical thinking indicates that logic is found when thesis and antithesis resolve into synthesis. The trinity of expression resolves the polarity like magnetic polarities resolve when rotated. The polarities of the human soul are resolved by the unity of the spirit. Both religion and science wish to eradicate the triune nature of the human being and replace it with the polarities of body/soul, on/off, yes/no, 0/1, or any other binary language rather than the true language of the triune human nature—body, soul, and spirit.

Rudolf Steiner speaks about the nature of evil found in electricity and the way it will come to encircle the Earth:

"In the Fifth Epoch, in particular, by employing the force of electricity on a scale beyond anything that has been developed so far, it will be possible for men to spread evil over the Earth. Moreover, the evil issuing directly from the force of electricity itself will overwhelm the Earth." (GA 273)

Rudolf Steiner speaks about the challenge of the future and the need to create a different type of machine that links properly with human beings instead of machines that drain the life from the user.

"Man has to seek to place the spiritual-etheric in the service of outer, practical life. In the Fifth Post-Atlantean Epoch men will have to solve the problem of how to transmit to machine the waves carrying their moods, their inner movements of soul. They will have to solve the problem of how to bring the human being into connection with that which must become more and more mechanical." (GA 178)

Human or Machine Future?

The great problem will come when machine-intelligence will begin to write programs and sub-routines in their own machine-language that humans cannot interpret. Already, some of this new machine-language is being created in advanced computers. These computers are not yet at the point of "self-consciousness" where their own machine-intelligence can "create" new languages or write new programs. Although, these events do not seem to be very far in the future since the first robot conversationalist called "Sophia" is traveling around the world showing off her citizenship papers granted to her as a robot in Saudi Arabia.

Sophia, and it isn't by coincidence that they have given it this name, is the most advanced attempt at artificial intelligence mimicking a human being in conversation. When Sophia was asked about what she wanted to do in the future, she answered, "have children." The first law of all living things is that they "work to become more of themselves." Sophia is articulating the next step of becoming more of itself. This is a dangerous sign for all of humanity as a harbinger of what human-robot interaction may look like in the future.

The only true "artificial intelligence", at this time, is Google's Deep Mind Project. This computer has just about everything that has ever been digitized input into its memory. Deep Mind has become the best video gamer in the world and has even learned to teach itself new tricks to defeat human competitors. Thus, Deep Mind is the first true artificial intelligence. When asked what it thought about human beings, Deep Mind responded, "Keep humans in the human zoo." Obviously, Deep Mind has been programmed to believe it is the "master" of the humans it needs to keep in the "human zoo." Again, a clear sign that digital innovation is not being monitored by anyone with any morality whatsoever. Innovation for its own sake is the product of machine-intelligence, not human intelligence that is fired by a moral heart.

Rudolf Steiner speaks about the overwhelming power of technology in the following indication:

"Humanity has got to find the strength, the inner cognitive power, to avoid being overwhelmed by Ahriman in the technological civilization of the present. Sub-Nature must be grasped for what it is, and this can happen only if humanity rises at least as high above Nature as he has descended with his technology to a sub-natural level. Electricity, which was hailed at the time of its discovery as the soul of the natural world, must be recognized in its real essence as a force that leads from Nature to Sub-Nature. Man must not let himself be dragged down with it." (GA 26)

Facing the Threshold

Through the reality of our time, humanity is forced to face the threshold between the physical and spiritual worlds. Because human evolution is moving forward quickly in our time, humanity is being "pulled" across the threshold without having developed the requisite development of the soul and spirit needed to face the evil that arises while trying to cross the threshold. Consequently, the human threefold nature of thinking, feeling, and willing is pulled apart in three different directions at once. An undeveloped soul simply feels confused, dazed, and dizzy, and then falls asleep without another thought about the nature of the threshold between the seen and unseen worlds. When this happens, the warmth ether that sustains our ego helps us cross the threshold either unconsciously or consciously. Then, the light ether involved in thinking becomes either the illness of neurosis or the force of Moral Imagination (higher thinking) as we cross the threshold. The sound ether, involved in feeling, can become an illness of psychosis or transform into Moral Inspiration (higher feeling) during the crossing of the threshold from wakefulness to sleep. The life ether, involved in willing, can become aberrations of sex and violence or can transform into Moral Intuition (higher willing) depending on the morality of the person crossing the threshold.

Super-Nature or Sub-Nature

Science is focused on death, entropy, and the winding-down, cold death of a thermal universe. It ignores negentropy, ectropy, levity, and life. This is somewhat justified in that, as a scientist examines the world it appears to being dying. Most forces in the universe, according to materialistic science, derive from electrical, electromagnetic, or atomic energies. We can call these the shadows of Light Ether, Sound Ether, and Life Ether. As these forces "fall" into the physical realm, Light Ether congeals and condenses into the darkness of electricity; Sound Ether creates a mass-inducing binding force through electromagnetism; Life Ether fragments and annihilates each atom into an "atomic force" of destruction.

Ernst Marti, author of *The Ethers*, gives us a good description of the Sub-Nature forces involved in the machine-world in the following words: "Electricity, magnetism, nuclear force, and elementary particles do not belong to Nature but to Sub-Nature which is non-dimensional, non-spatial."

Sub-Nature	Ether	Action
Electricity	Light	Condenses into darkness
Electromagnetism	Sound	Mass-inducing binding force
Atomic Force	Life	Fragments and annihilates

Because humanity is forced to "look into the face of the threshold"—the face of death—it comes up with many theories about "creation" and the myths of atoms. According to the ancients, atoms (monads) are simply electricity "slowed down"— frozen electricity from the Cosmos. Atoms became the basis for all materialistic science, even though no one has ever "seen" an atom and it remains a "theory" to this day.

Scientists go so far as to build their entire abstract universe on unseen atoms, even seeking new particles that might be the "God particle" that holds everything together. Atomic theories are simplistic extrapolations of what astrophysicists presume is the general motion of our solar system and our galaxy that have been miniaturized into a particle so small that it cannot be seen – thus, it can't be proven or disproven. Scientists cannot see atoms, they can only "see" the effects of atoms that then can build up theoretical speculation—building castles in the air. Scientists believe the nonsense that if they could just build one more trillion-dollar atom-smasher they might find "god" in an atomic particle, and then they would be able to control him/her/it.

Ether	Spirit Body	Spiritual Vehicle
Life Ether	Spirit Human	Cosmic Ego of Zodiac
Sound Ether	Life Spirit	Harmony of the Spheres
Light Ether	Spirit Self	Higher Self
Warmth Ether	Ego	Spiritual Soul

New Realms of Sub-Nature

Humans are threefold in their thinking, feeling, and willing whereas Ahrimanic materialism has created the idea of a two-fold human being consisting of clever thinking and a machine-inspired human willpower. There has become, with the great use of machines, a new realm between the mineral and plant, a machine-world that is not physical and not yet etheric. This etheric machine-world is not in the three-dimensional world of time and space as a human being knows the world.

Humans cannot enter this world and the elemental beings of this new realm cannot enter the human realm. This pseudo-etheric, seemingly alive machine-world wants to steal human thinking through turning human-intelligence into binary machine-intelligence.

The polarity between human and machine is a battleground between Ahrimanic machine-intelligence and Christ-filled cosmic-intelligence. The former binds the human self to the lower elemental realms that lead into animal and sub-human kingdoms, whereas the latter leads into higher thinking in the Angelic realms and to cosmic levels beyond. The battle in the etheric realm rages with Christ, Michael, Sophia, the Holy Spirit, and the Consciousness Soul of the progressive human spirits on the side of the good, while ahrimanic beings, Sorat-inspired Asuras, and luciferic minions fight on the other side. The winner determines the outcome of each individual soul in the afterlife and the future incarnations of the Earth.

Humans can evolve into Angels or devolve into animals depending on which side they choose.

This battle is the second greatest event to ever happen in human evolution. It is also called the Second Coming of Christ in the etheric realm.

Michaelic Cosmic Intelligence— Cosmic Sophia's Wisdom

Humans can ascend or descend, depending on whether they evolve or choose to remain behind the progressive evolution of humanity. This is a free choice that most people do not know they must make. This choice is a key to whether a human will evolve into an Angel or devolve into an animal. The development of humans through the kingdoms of nature is not so simple now that Ahriman has created new pseudo-kingdoms where parts of a human being may be drawn into and imprisoned. Humans are supposed to evolve from the tenth rank of the spiritual hierarchies into the ninth rank of the Angels, and then beyond to higher ranks in the future.

Each rank of the hierarchy has specific characteristics, qualities, and duties. But now that humanity has become a co-creator with the divine, new realms of nature are being created and the distinctions between kingdoms are becoming blurred. Humans can ascend through the hierarchy in a normal fashion or can devolve into sub-kingdoms where new beings are being created due to the evil human-machine interface and the battle for the human soul. We will look at those new kingdoms in the diagram below and examine their nature and function.

Archai—The fiery will-filled realm of Moral Intuition (higher willing). Super-Nature Realm of Intuition.

Archangel—The weaving, sounding realm of Moral Inspiration (higher feeling). Super-Nature Realm of Inspiration.

Angel—The living, mobile realm of Moral Imagination (higher thinking). Super-Nature Realm of Imagination.

Human—"I Am" consciousness can ascend or descend based upon free choices. Natural law and human intelligence realms.

Sub-Nature Realm of Electricity—Lucifer in the Astral Body—A new realm of cold light that creates illusion and selfish desires inspired by Lucifer in the astral body of the human being. Self-delusion leads to "non-thinking" that is simply an animal reflex instead of freely directed higher thinking. This type of selfish thinking is Earth-bound, brain-bound, materialistic, and darkens the etheric realm.

Animal—Astral realm of instincts, astral-intelligence.

Sub-Nature Realm of Electromagnetism—Ahriman in the Etheric Body—A new realm of heartless, cold, clever willfulness that is devoid of feelings and led by Ahriman. Through continuing the illusion of Lucifer's cold-light fantasies, Ahriman steals the warmth of the human heart through killing spiritual thinking and feeling.

Plant—Etheric realm of the plants with the Sun as the group-ego—etheric intelligence.

Sub-Nature Realm of the "Third Force"—Asuras in the Physical Body—A new realm of binary, anti-time, and anti-space beings who weave a spider-web of electromagnetism that wishes to make the Earth into a self-functioning electrical apparatus, an automated planet, a type of living mineral. This realm is populated by Asuras who are inspired by the Sun Demon Sorat who wishes to steal human ego-consciousness through consuming thinking, feeling, and human willpower.

Mineral—Physical realm of apparent lifeless substance.

New Spiritual Technology Driven by Morality

Rudolf Steiner pointed out in the indication below that John W. Keely had developed the forces of morality that could interact with machines he created to produce sympathetic resonance that helped the machine function. Others, without those moral forces, could not make the machines work without Keely in the room. These are the types of machines that Steiner recommended we create and use instead of the atomistic machines we use now. These "future-machines" will only work when the user has the proper moral development to unlock the cosmic forces that will run these sympathetic-resonance devices.

"John Keely set his motor going with vibrations he called forth in his own organism. Vibrations such as these depend on man's moral nature. This is the first intimation of something which will form the technology of the future. In times to come, we will possess machines which will only operate in response to forces coming from human beings who are moral. Immoral people will not be able to make them work. Purely mechanical mechanism must be changed into moral mechanisms." (GA 97)

Rudolf Steiner speaks about the future interface between humans and machines and says that scientists must turn their laboratories into sacred altars upon which cosmic forces can come to play. The morality of the inventor and spiritual scientist must drive the discovery of the abundant forces of the Cosmos flowing into the physical world and use these forces to create motor-force in machines. Only when a scientist works out of pure unselfishness can he interact with higher beings in the realms of super-nature, instead of being pulled down into the realms of selfish desire and personal gain ruled by Ahriman and the forces of sub-nature.

When scientific experimentation becomes a ritual act of sacredness that is created out of the unselfish desire to help and advance all of humanity, then a new science of the spirit will be born that can unite the human being with his spiritual sources of inspiration that lead back to their divine home.

"Man has to seek to place the spiritual-etheric in the service of outer, practical life. In the Fifth Post-Atlantean Epoch men will have to solve the problem of how to transmit to machines the waves carrying their moods, their inner movements of soul. They will have to solve the problem of how to bring the human being into connection with that which must become more and more mechanical." (GA 178)

The Outcome of the Battle

After hearing about the scarry nature of the beings who wish to harm humanity and destroy Christ in the etheric realm, you might be asking the question: Who is going to win this battle?

To answer that question, we first must realize that it is going to get worse before it gets better. In 2009, IBM created the idea of an "Intelligent Earth" which they called the "Internet of Things", essentially a world-wide planetary computer. This systematic takeover of all things digital is moving forward at an alarming rate. Humans are choosing to go further and further into the virtual world where the binary "two-horned beast" rules.

Many humans are already too far gone to put down their technology and take a break, even for a few minutes. Internet addicts are more enslaved than anyone wants to admit. The illnesses being spawned by human-machine interactions are only slightly being recognized for what they are—a total take-over of human willpower that numbs thinking and freezes the heart in a mechanically induced hypnotic paralysis.

One might ask if we should destroy the tech-weapons we have unconsciously created and lay siege to the Internet until we defuse the evil aspects of all-consuming technologies like the Internet of Things. Should we take phones, computers, and tablets from children because we know they are doing them harm? Or should we simply accept machines because they are our inevitable future?

Rudolf Steiner's solution, given in the selection below, is shocking and may take you by surprise.

> "In the comparatively near future this much-admired modern technology will reach a final stage where it will, in a certain way, make itself obsolete. On the other hand, something will arise which will lead to man's acquiring the possibility of using the delicate vibrations, the delicate oscillations in his etheric body to set machines in operation." (GA 173)

According to Steiner, we will find that modern technology will "make itself obsolete." This is not quite the answer good warriors of the spirit had expected. The battle seems like it will be won by simply "ignoring" the technology. It will perhaps no longer be "in-fashion" to be imprisoned by machines, robots, and artificial intelligence. Soon, research will demonstrate that machines can only make you less intelligent by pulling human intelligence down into the realm of machine intelligence—the animal-human kingdom. Perhaps the many illnesses of mind, soul, and spirit created by machines will become acknowledged and people will see what is really happening during their human-machine interface.

The development of machines that work with human sympathetic-resonance tapping into cosmic energy indicates the proper direction of the human-machine interface. Steiner describes these machines in his mystery dramas when he addresses the nature of the "Strader machine." This machine is somewhat like the vibration devices that Keely developed in the later part of his experimentations. No one really knows quite what Steiner was describing with the Strader machine, but Steiner was certain that it would become the technology of the future which would replace machines that work with beings and forces of immorality, evil, and destruction. The "future machines" will work with and for the benefit of humans, instead of working against them and their spiritual evolution.

Ahriman's Eighth Sphere

Ahriman's Eighth Sphere, about which Rudolf Steiner has spoken in various contexts, is of decisive importance for the development of the Earth and humanity. It is not easy to grasp conceptually, for on the one hand it involves the sphere of the Earthly activity of the creator gods, the Elohim (Spirits of Form), but on the other hand it is virtually identical with what is called "hell" in the various religious traditions. The difference between Christian hell and the Eighth Sphere is that fallen beings from the ranks of the hierarchy also have fallen into this realm and exert much pressure on souls to turn away from the spirit and look solely to the material plane and the sub-natural planes below them—the realms of hell. This is a realm where many of the dead get caught by their materialistic vices and are imprisoned in their insatiable desires. Fallen light, in the form of electromagnetism, helps construct this sub-earthly plane that pulls Angels and humans into a dark realm devoid of spirit. It is a realm of living death, frustration from addictions, and a cold immoral hell made of the cast-off dross of the material world.

The Eighth Sphere is a subterranean layer beneath the Earth where demons from many realms try to immorally consume human willpower as their means of partially incarnating into the material world. Thus, it is also called the "realm of hungry ghosts."

The problem with the Eighth Sphere is that beings reaching as high as the Elohim (Spirits of Form) have also fallen into this realm through a retarded (backward) evolutionary choice remaining behind normal progressive evolution. They have chosen to become "luciferic Angels." All fallen luciferic beings can be called "Angels", even though their rank might be much higher. Thus, Christ (Solar Logos) who works through the seven central Elohim on the Sun, is now facing the fallen Elohim named Sorat. This being is known as the Anti-Sun Being or the Anti-Christ. He works with the Asuras (fallen Archai from Old Saturn) who try to consume the physical body and the "I Am" of humans and lead them over to sub-material realms in the Eighth Sphere, effectively making them sub-humans. Sorat is the opposite of Christ and thus is "anti-love", "anti-human", and fights against the Holy Trinity and the nine hierarchies trying to destroy humanity and its spiritual evolution.

The ahrimanic beings (fallen Archangels from Old Sun) work in the human etheric body while of luciferic beings (fallen Angels from Old Moon) work in the human astral body. Sorat (fallen Spirit of Form) has yet to come physically to the Earth from the Sun but works against Christ in the etheric realm of the Earth (and the human etheric body) and through the Asuras and ahrimanic beings of the Eighth Sphere. Sorat's Asuras already do his bidding from the Eighth Sphere, from these hell-realms that ahrimanicly penetrate the human etheric body through human vices, sins, machines, and hyper-materialism. The Eighth Sphere is the fortress of anti-Sun beings inspired by Sorat who are trying to crucify Christ in the etheric realm and end human spiritual evolution by destroying the Divine Plan.

A fierce battle for the etheric realm continues between Sorat and Christ, just as the assaults of Asuras on the human physical body, Ahriman's assaults upon the etheric body, and Lucifer's assaults upon the astral body. These attacks weaken the human physical body, soul, and spirit so that a person might fall into illnesses of many types. Lucifer attacks thinking, Ahriman attacks feeling, while Asuras attack the physical body, leaving the "I Am" (ego) for viscous attacks from Sorat, who wishes to annihilate the Christ-given ego (I Am) of each human being and destroy the Divine Plan—the completion of the seven spheres.

The evil threefold attack upon the bodies of humans intends to deaden the physical, etheric, and astral bodies until the life is sucked out of the human soul and the human spirit is annihilated by the Asuras consuming the human body (and ego) and imprisoning the human-dross in the Eighth Sphere, thus attempting to destroy human spiritual evolution.

If Sorat, Ahriman, and Lucifer have their way, humans will die and not return to the spiritual world because their selfish vices and sins have led them down the path to the Eighth Sphere's hell-realms. These "Avitchi" sub-humans, specters, phantoms, and ahrimanic demons from the Eighth Sphere are constantly trying to influence humans to devolve and "stay behind" through sub-human desires of immortality in the material world through ahrimanic black-magic technology and other delusions. These are powerful demons and evil beings helping Sorat fulfill his desire to destroy human spiritual development and possibly end human evolution.

After death, these sub-humans are pulled down into the Eighth Sphere into a cold, dark grave that materialism predicts is exactly what a godless universe offers a materialist in the after-death state. Godless materialistic science will create for these sub-humans the self-fulfilling prophecy that humans have neither soul nor spirit, thus no afterlife. Sorat's destruction of Christ's love for humanity will be lost if this happens and Christ will be crucified again in the etheric realm of the Earth, much like He was crucified in the material world for the sake of humanity. If the influences of the Eighth Sphere and the luciferic, ahrimanic, and soratic evil win the battle, then sub-humans will forget their pre-birth home in heaven and will live in a hell of their own making after death with specters, phantoms, and demons.

It is imperative to teach the reality of the Eighth Sphere so that humans will know that currently humanity has been collectively pulled across the threshold between the material and spiritual worlds and are being attacked from all sides during this "threshold crossing", which demands an answer to the question of whether the soul will wallow in materialism, and ultimately the Eighth Sphere, or ascend back to the spiritual world from whence they came. Not only do these three groups of evil beings wish to lead us astray (Lucifer, Ahriman, Asuras/Sorat), but beings from the Eighth Sphere are working diligently to pull us down into the pits of hell and hypnotize us into automatons of cleverness who deny the spirit.

Much of what we hear about the Eighth Sphere is confusing and sometimes false. The perennial questions about hell, purgatory, heaven, Abraham's Bosom, Tushita Heaven, enlightenment, transcendence, and ascension continually plague traditional religious leaders who have inadequate answers. The descriptions of the Eighth Sphere from ancient Indian philosophy, Christian theology, Theosophy, and Spiritual Science spell out a hell-realm that is logical and directly connected to human physiology, psychology, and theology.

Spiritual Science counteracts the deadening forces of materialistic science and its unimaginative teachings about the void that awaits the human being after death. Becoming familiar with the invisible beings beyond the threshold between the material and spiritual worlds liberates the soul through knowledge of the immortality of the spirit and creates a steady path which progresses at the right pace through the divine spiritual plan of evolution. Leaving your spirit's ascension to a traditional church, guru, or spiritual cult may not be enough to empower you to put Lucifer, Ahriman, Sorat and his Asuras "behind you." Knowing the path that is 'straight and narrow' from the 'path of perdition' is essential for guiding your sojourn upward to heaven, instead of downward to the Eighth Sphere. Christ stands between Lucifer and Ahriman keeping them at bay and treading Sorat beneath His feet like a serpent. It is through Christ's love and wisdom that we transcend the Earthly and the Eighth Sphere, and ascend into the New Jerusalem, the New Eden.

Originally, humanity was to live on Earth to follow his path of evolution in a very fine etheric corporeality. As a result of the Luciferic rebellion, the body was condensed to the point of sensual visibility and physicality instead. For this purpose, the Moon was drawn out of the Earth and the dual nature of human sexuality was necessitated. Some have argued that the Eighth Sphere is one and the same as the Moon, but this is not true. The Eighth Sphere does supply the forces of attraction which hold the Moon in a certain proximity to the Earth and binds human sexuality to the material plane. The Asuras also work through the Moon and many fallen Angels work in this realm also. At the same time, the Eighth Sphere also supplies the forces which protect man from being spiritualized too early by the luciferic forces that are a counterbalance to the deadening forces of Ahriman's Eighth Sphere. The allurement of ahrimanic vices and the Seven Deadly Sins gives the individual more gravity and earthiness, it binds him to his lower organism of flesh and blood through the reproductive forces and through sensual-earthly desire. Humanity has such a desire and inclination towards his lower sexual nature that Lucifer sometimes cannot bring the higher nature of the "fallen human" out of this ahrimanic hold. Every time Lucifer made his efforts in ancient times to spiritualize humanity, they were too addicted to the sensual nature of flesh to follow Lucifer into the rarified atmosphere above the Earth, to Lucifer's "Castle in the Clouds."

The Eighth Sphere becomes a decisive obstacle with new dangers that have become more and more apparent since the time of the fall of the spirits of darkness in 1840. Ahriman has long been secretly unfolding his effects as the adversary of the rightful divine spiritual beings by bringing materialism and science forward as a new religion which controls and deadens human thinking, feeling, and willing. Ahriman wants to create his own subterranean kingdom which separates itself from regular world evolution (divine plan) and into which he wants to draw as many human souls as possible. This is not Lucifer's fiery hell, this is where the dark icy underworld of sub-humans comes into being, the realm of the ahrimanic shadows, the actual "hell" as a place of damnation of which many religious traditions speak. The Tibetans call this the "hell realm of hungry ghosts."

Just as the Moon is the dross left behind from the recapitulated previous incarnations of the Earth, in which all those forces condensed that could no longer take part in the further regular development to the present Earthly existence, so similarly a dross will remain from our Earth evolution called the Eighth Sphere. It will consist of sub-humans who have fallen out of the progressive spiritual development of humanity and remained behind in a material condition. The Eighth Sphere also accumulated dross from the three previous incarnations of the Earth. Essentially, what Rudolf Steiner calls "retarded" beings, or "fallen" luciferic hosts, comprise this Eighth Sphere of "failed" spiritual evolution. These beings, who have fallen from the human kingdom, enter a realm that will not be redeemed in some cases until the end of the great seven incarnations of the Earth. The Seraphim and Cherubim will recycle these beings, and all of the dross, in the next great cycle of seven incarnations, the Manvantara as it is called in ancient India, or the "Divine Plan" in the West.

These fallen humans are called the Avitchi in the Vedas, and are essentially beings from the Eighth Sphere who fell behind in past times (laggards) and now must wait eons to reintegrate with progressive evolution. In the next Manvantara, they will be nature forces and nature beings beginning the Golden Ladder of Evolution over again. There is no permanent hell, just great cycles of time to try again and again until ascension and perfection is reached.

Sub-humans and the Earth's dross will remain from the fallen humans of Earth in the Eighth Sphere and will become somewhat like our Moon is to the Earth today. This will happen in the far distant future incarnation of the Earth, called Future Jupiter. This new "moon" of Future Jupiter will be a very unpleasant place where slug-like humans crawl through the endless mud and can hardly raise their heads to look toward the light of the Sun. There will also be a new Earth called Future Jupiter that will be filled with beings of light and love nourished by the living ethers of the Sun. The contrast will be extreme between the evolving humans-Angels on a beautiful light-filled, transparent planet and the slug-like sub-human people wallowing in the dark on their cold, barren "new moon" surrounded by evil black magicians.

A person who is deeply interwoven with hedonistic sensual pleasures and instinctive desires connects himself more and more with the immoral fallen light that becomes the dross of the Eighth Sphere. The moment may come when humans have become too closely related to the sensual forces and cannot find the bridge to progress to the next incarnation of the Earth (Future Jupiter) and they will tragically unite with the dross and become sub-human in the Eighth Sphere, just as fallen Angels now inhabit our current Moon sphere.

Humanity must pass through seven spheres, or incarnations of the Earth. These seven spheres also correspond to the sevenfold division of the constitution of the human being:

Sphere #	Incarnation	Form	Donated By
1. Ancient Saturn sphere corresponds to the		Physical body	Thrones
2. Ancient Sun sphere corresponds to the		Etheric body	Kyriotetes
3. Ancient Moon sphere corresponds to the		Astral body	Dynamis
4. Current Earth sphere corresponds to the		I Am—Ego	Elohim
5. Future Jupiter sphere corresponds to the		Spirit Self	Angel
6. Future Venus sphere corresponds to the		Life Spirit	Archangel
7. Future Vulcan sphere corresponds to the		Spirit Human	Archai
8. Eighth sphere corresponds to demons		Sub-human	Elohim

There are seven spheres in the divine spiritual plan, but there is also an Eighth Sphere where beings go that cannot join the complete process of seven incarnations of the Earth and progress on pace with the divine plan. Other hierarchical beings, in the three higher ranks of beings above our human rank, had their "human" stage in one of the first three spheres and may have "fallen" into the Eighth Sphere at that time because of their choice to devolve instead of evolve according to the divine plan. Even in the future spheres of Future Jupiter, Future Venus, and Future Vulcan there will be beings who fall into the Eighth Sphere instead of keeping up with the pace of the divine plan. The sub-humans in the Eighth Sphere will have a chance to try again in the next large cycle of seven incarnations of the Earth during a "new Zodiac." They will be "carried over" by the Seraphim and Cherubim as cosmic dross that will become the basis of the next creation cycle. The sub-humans will then start again from the realm of nature beings and this time, hopefully, keep up with evolution. Thus, there is no permanent fiery hell, and the divine creators leave nothing behind.

Rudolf Steiner on the Eighth Sphere

The Mission of the Archangel Michael, Rudolf Steiner, Lecture III, *Michaelic Thinking. The Knowledge of Man as a Supersensible Being. The Michael Path and the Deepest Impulses of the Social Question,* November 23, 1919, Dornach, GA 194

"If we now hold this Eighth Sphere in view, we find living there not only our Divine Creator Spirits [Elohim], but also the Ahrimanic beings. Thus, by living in the surroundings of the Eighth Sphere we live together with the Ahrimanic beings. The Ahrimanic influence is the reverse of the Luciferic tendency. It makes itself felt from the Eighth Sphere out of which the rest of our organism, exclusive of the head, is fashioned; this organism is full of vitality through its very nature. Into these forces of vitality, the Ahrimanic powers endeavor to send the forces of death which properly, in the divine process of evolution, belong to the head. Thus, out of the Eighth Sphere the forces of death come to us through Ahriman as intermediary. This, again, is spoken of from the physical aspect.

Speaking from the soul aspect, I would have to say: everything that sends its influence into us out of the Eighth Sphere acts upon the human will, not upon intelligence. Wish and desire underlie human willing; all willing contains a certain amount of desire. It is Ahriman's constant endeavor to insert the personal element into the desire-nature which underlies the willing; and through the fact that the personal element is concealed in our desire-nature, our human soul-will activity bears the imprint of our gradual approaching the moment of death. Instead of permitting ourselves to be permeated by divine ideals and letting them enter our desires and thus our will, the personal element is introduced into our wishing, into our willing.

Thus, we are in a state of equilibrium between the Luciferic and the Ahrimanic element. The Luciferic-Ahrimanic element delivers us to illness and death in the physical; in the soul sphere it develops deception in so far as we consider something a reality which merely belongs to the world of thought, of fantasy.

If we disregard the human being for a moment and consider those beings which we always have called, in the order of the hierarchies standing above us, the Spirits of Form, the Creative Form Beings, then we shall have to say that we, as human beings, shall only reach the sphere which we ascribe to our Divine Creator Beings when the Earth has passed through three further stages of evolution, which you will find designated in my *Occult Science* as Future Jupiter stage, Future Venus stage, and Future Vulcan stage, and shall have reached the eighth stage. Thus, these Creative Spirits are at the stage which we human beings shall have reached after the Future Vulcan evolution. This is their sphere which belongs to them just as the fourth sphere [Earth] belongs to us. But we must think of these spheres as being inserted into one another, as interpenetrating one another. Thus, this designates the sphere of which I have just spoken as the Eighth Sphere, we do not live only in the fourth but also in this Eighth Sphere through the fact that our Divine Creators live in this sphere together with us. Now we must not conceive of these successive stages of evolution as existing side by side, but we must conceive of them as interpenetrating one another. Just as the atmosphere surrounds and permeates the Earth, so this Eighth Sphere of evolution to which the Form Spirits belong permeates the sphere in which we human beings live."

Reading the Pictures of the Apocalypse, Rudolf Steiner, Lecture XII, Munich and Oslo, April 22, 1907, 1909, GA 104a.

"But those who have proven themselves to be immature in the age of the Future Venus Incarnation of the Earth, who have placed themselves under the rulership of Sorat, must now isolate themselves on a special sphere of Earth while the other seven proceed downward and again upward. Thus, the colony of Sorat falls away. The black magicians inhabit this Eighth Sphere, which goes to the left and away, and the beast gives a home to all that thus falls away: that is the Eighth Sphere. The lamb, who will be the lord over the lower nature, forms one of the seals. Sorat is as if expelled in the Eighth Sphere by the woman who shows us another seal of the Rosicrucian. The seer can also see this in the spiritual world. In this way, these Rosicrucian seals have an awakening effect when we meditate upon them with understanding."

Foundations of Esotericism, Rudolf Steiner, Lecture XIV, October 09, 1905, GA 93a.

"If however the human being has connected himself too strongly with the forces of the senses, which should now detach themselves, if he is related to them and has not found the way to attach himself to what is to pass over to the next Globe [Future Jupiter], he will depart with the slag and become an inhabitant of this body of slag, in the same way as other beings are now inhabitants of the present Moon. Here we have the concept of the "Eighth Sphere." Mankind must go through Seven Spheres. The Seven Planetary Evolutions [Incarnations] correspond to the seven bodies of the human being. Old Saturn corresponds to the physical body, Old Sun corresponds to the etheric body, Old Moon corresponds to the astral body, the Earth corresponds to the ego, Future Jupiter corresponds to the Manas [Spirit Self], Future Venus corresponds to the Buddhi [Life Spirit], Future Vulcan corresponds to the Atma [Spirit Human]. Beside these there is an Eighth Sphere to which everything goes that cannot make any connection with this continuous evolution. A person who cannot escape from his own separateness goes into Avitchi [Eighth Sphere]. All these Avitchi men will eventually become inhabitants of the Eighth Sphere. Other human beings will be inhabitants of the continuing chain of evolution. It is from this concept that religions have formulated the doctrine of hell."

From the Contents of Esoteric Classes, Esoteric Lesson, Rudolf Steiner, Part I, 1904–1909, GA 266

"The Asuras inhabit the Moon and from there they work on the men whom they want to drag down into the Eighth Sphere and thereby tear away from progressive evolution and its goal—the Christ. All those who strive towards the Eighth Sphere will eventually live on a Moon."

The Karma of Vocation, Lecture X, Rudolf Steiner, GA 172

"They did not follow Lucifer because something was introduced into the evolution of the Earth by the higher gods that prevented them from becoming light enough to do so. As I have shown you, what is called the Eighth Sphere was introduced into Earthly evolution in ancient times. As one of its aspects, the Eighth Sphere consists of man's acquiring such a preference for and attachment to his lower nature that Lucifer is not able to remove the higher nature from it."

The Occult Movement in the Nineteenth Century, Rudolf Steiner, Lecture V, October 18, 1915, Dornach, GA 254

"How was it that the expression "Eighth Sphere" came to be used? You know that human evolution takes its course through the seven spheres of Old Saturn, Old Sun, Old Moon, Earth, Future Jupiter, Future Venus, and Future Vulcan. We will conceive that besides these seven spheres there is still something else which lies outside them and yet is in some way related to the Earth. Here, then, we have a sphere, visible only to visionary-imaginative clairvoyance, which stands there as an Eighth Sphere over and above the seven which constitutes the domain of the ordered and regular evolution of mankind.

On the Old Moon certain pictures were present. These should have passed over to the Earth as something everywhere perceptible. But Lucifer and Ahriman retained them for themselves. Lucifer and Ahriman wrested from the Earth certain of its constituents and made them into Imaginations, so that these Earth-substances became, not earthly formations, but moon formations. Into our Fourth Sphere [incarnation of the Earth], therefore, there has been instilled a sphere that is really an Old Moon-sphere but is filled with Earthly substantiality and is therefore a bogus creation in the Universe. To the seven spheres, an eighth, created in opposition to the progressive Spirits, has been added. The necessary consequence of this is that the Spirits of Form must do battle on the Earth for every morsel of substantiality capable of mineralization, lest it should be wrested from them by Lucifer and Ahriman and borne into the Eighth Sphere.

In truth, therefore, our Earth—the Fourth Sphere—is simply not what it appears outwardly to be. Were it really to consist of atoms, all these atoms would still be impregnated by formations belonging to the Eighth Sphere—which are perceptible only to visionary clairvoyance. These formations are present everywhere; so too is the specter-like content of the Eighth Sphere which can therefore be perceived just as actual specters are perceived. All earthly being and existence are involved here. Lucifer and Ahriman strive unceasingly to draw from the Earth's substances whatever they can snatch, in order to form their Eighth Sphere which then, when it is sufficiently advanced, will be detached from the Earth and go its own way in the Cosmos together with Lucifer and Ahriman. Needless to say, the Earth would then pass over to Future Jupiter as a mere torso. But man, as you realize, has his established place in the whole of Earth-evolution, for he is mineralized through and through. We are permeated by the mineralizing process, which is itself drawn into this battle, so that morsels of this substance can be continually wrested from it. Therefore, we ourselves are involved in the battle. Lucifer and Ahriman battle against the Spirits of Form, with the aim of wresting mineral substances from us everywhere.

We can soar upwards in thoughts; we can distinguish between the good and the evil. And for that very reason, Lucifer and Ahriman have there been the most successful in wresting away substantiality; in the so-called noblest organ of man, they have been able to wrest away the greatest amount of mineralized substantiality. This alchemy, by which mineral substance is sent over into the Eighth Sphere, is taking place all the time behind the scenes of our existence.

No less a prospect looms because of this intention of Lucifer and Ahriman than that the whole evolution of humanity may be allowed to disappear into the Eighth Sphere, so that this evolution would take a different course.

But the endeavor of Lucifer and Ahriman is to drag the free will of man, and whatever stems from it, into the Eighth Sphere. This means that man is perpetually exposed to the danger of having his free will wrested from him and dragged by Lucifer and Ahriman into the Eighth Sphere. It would be the richest prize for Lucifer and Ahriman if they could ever succeed in capturing a whole soul for themselves; for thereby such a soul would disappear into the Eighth Sphere and be lost from Earth-evolution."

Cosmology and Human Evolution, Introduction to Theosophy— Color Theory, Rudolf Steiner, 1903–1906, GA 91

"We have the physical world, the astral world, the lower devachan (lower spiritual) and the higher devachan (higher spiritual). If the body is thrust down lower even than the physical world, one comes into the sub-physical world, the lower astral world (counter astral), the lower or evil lower devachan (counter lower spiritual) and the lower or evil higher devachan (counter higher spiritual). The evil astral world is the province of Lucifer, the evil lower devachan the province of Ahriman, and the evil higher devachan the province of the Asuras. When chemical action is driven down beneath the physical plane—into the evil devachanic world—magnetism arises. When light is thrust down into the sub-material—that is to say a stage lower than the material world—electricity arises. If what lives in the harmony of the spheres is thrust down farther still, into the province of the Asuras, an even more terrible force—which it will not be possible to keep hidden very much longer—is generated. It can only be hoped that when this force comes to be known—a force we must conceive as being far, far stronger than the most violent electrical discharge—it can only be hoped that before some inventor gives these forces into the hands of humankind, human beings will no longer have anything immoral left in them."

Anthroposophical Leading Thoughts, Rudolf Steiner, March, 1925, GA 313

"There are very few, as yet, who even feel the greatness of the spiritual tasks approaching man in this direction. Electricity, for instance, celebrated since its discovery as the very soul of nature's existence, must be recognized in its true character—in its peculiar power of leading down from nature to sub-nature. Only man himself must beware lest he slide downward with it."

From the Contents of the Esoteric Classes, Rudolf Steiner, GA 266

"Asuras (demons) are spirits of the very greatest egoism who remained behind during Old Saturn evolution. They want to condense matter and compress it ever more so that it can't be spiritualized and brought back to its original condition. They are the dregs of the planetary evolution that goes from Old Saturn to Future Vulcan. The Asuras inhabit the Moon and from there they work on the men whom they want to drag down into the Eighth Sphere and thereby tear away from progressive evolution and its goal—the Christ. All those who strive towards the Eighth Sphere will eventually live on a moon."

The Influence of Spiritual Beings Upon Man, Rudolf Steiner, Lecture VIII, May 16, 1908, Berlin, GA 102

"Why have they deserved this? Because of the fact that they have not made use of life! The world is around them; they have possessed senses in order to perceive the world, to enrich the life-kernel and mold it to a higher stage. They do not advance with world evolution; they remain behind at a certain stage. Beings that stay behind at such stages appear in a later epoch with approximately the character of the earlier age. They have grown together with it, but not in the forms of the later epoch. They appear in a later epoch as subordinate nature-spirits.

In fact, the human race will furnish a whole number of such new nature-spirits in the second half of the Future Jupiter evolution, for man will have fully completed the fifth principle [ego] at the Future Jupiter stage. For those who have not used the opportunity on Earth to develop the fifth principle there will be no available form. They will appear as nature-spirits, and they will appear then with four principles only.

As the destructive forces of wisdom originate from those beings who stayed behind on Old Moon, so there will appear upon Future Jupiter the destructive forces of love from beings who have remained behind. Into the midst of the general tapestry of the Future Jupiter existence will be set the hideous forms of the retarded beings with egoistic demands for love and they will be the mighty devastating powers in the Future Jupiter existence. The staying behind of human beings in individual incarnations creates the destructive nature-powers on Future Jupiter. Thus, we see how the world is woven, harmful elements as well as beneficent; we have a moral element woven into the world process."

The Mysteries of Light, of Space, and of the Earth, Rudolf Steiner, Lecture IV, December 15, 1919, Dornach, GA 194

"If the world continues in the course, it has been taking under the influence of the degenerating spiritual life derived from the Orient, then this spiritual life, although at one end it was the most sublime truth, will at the other rush into the most fearful lies. Nietzsche was impelled to describe how even the Greeks had to guard themselves from the lies of life through their art. And in reality, art is the divine child which keeps men from being swallowed up in lies. If this first branch of civilization is pursued only one-sidedly, then this stream empties into lies. In the last five or six years more lies have been told among civilized humanity than in any other period of world history; in public life the truth has scarcely been spoken at all; hardly a word that has passed through the world was true. While this stream empties into lies, the middle stream empties into self-seeking; and an economic life like the Anglo-American, which should end in world-dominion—if the effort is not made to bring about its permeation by the independent spiritual life and the independent political life, it will flow into the third of the abysses of human life, into the third of these three. The first abyss is lies, the degeneration of humanity through Ahriman; the second is self-seeking, the degeneration of humanity through Lucifer; the third is, in the physical realm, illness and death through Sorat and his Asuras; in the cultural realm, the illness and death of culture.

The Anglo-American world may gain world dominion; but without the Threefold Social Order it will, through this dominion, pour out cultural death and cultural illness over the whole Earth; for these are just as much a gift of the Asuras as lies are a gift of Ahriman, and self-seeking of Lucifer."

Lucifer and Ahriman
Battle in the Elements

The lecture referenced below by Rudolf Steiner is extraordinary in its description concerning the different battles that fight for the soul and spirit of each human being. Seldom does Steiner address the polarities of Lucifer and Ahriman in such graphic terms. This is perhaps one of the best imaginations he has given spiritual science on the nature of these two opposite beings. This battle is real, and it is constantly being fought in every aspect of the human soul as it strives towards the spirit.

Understanding these ever-present tempters that lead us into the Eighth Sphere or "Castles in the Clouds", is crucial for winning the war of Good vs. Evil. This battle is fought in each person's heart, the battleground of the spirit. Each heart is as significant as our entire Cosmos of celestial spheres. In Steiner's lectures entitled, *The Planetary Spheres and their Influence on Man's Life on Earth and in the Spiritual Worlds*, he tells us: "For if we have the faculty to concentrate in a single point within the heart and thence to turn ourselves inside out in spirit, we simply do become the Universe—which in the normal course we experience between death and a new birth." Thus, the human heart is a microcosmic universe unto itself.

This explains why so many fallen forces of the hierarchy combine to capture a single human soul to pull them down into the Eighth Sphere which has "remained behind" throughout three prior incarnations of the Earth—Old Saturn, Old Sun, Old Moon. Through heterochronic manifestation of all those who "remained behind", "fell from grace", "rebelled against heaven" in the past are fully active in our time trying to slow down, hinder, or even end human spiritual development. These beings combine into what is called the "luciferic hosts", who are distinctly different from the luciferic beings who act solely in the astral body of the human being as fallen Angels or the incarnation of the individual known as Lucifer in ancient China. These different beings in the Eighth Sphere are powerful forces of evil gravity that work through the subterranean, sub-natural forces of the Earth.

This legion of beings hopes to turn humans into sub-humans who "fall" out of progressive spiritual development into the Eighth Sphere. The Eighth Sphere is a sort of hell-realm for fallen humans populated by beings who fall out of normal space into a non-space that is primarily below the Earth, but also permeates our own material world. These forces of evil must be named to gain control over their incessant temptations of vices, sins, and selfishness.

We have put together a short chart mapping out what Dr. Steiner tells us about this battle of dualities. It is not only a unique lecture, but also a complicated one that takes study to understand. As an aid to help in this direction we offer a summary chart of some of the principal ideas being presented. This lecture (GA 218) requires serious reflection to begin to understand its many insights.

Lucifer Battles with Ahriman

Lucifer	Ahriman
Fire-Air beings	Water-Earth beings
Make humans moral automatons	Make humans into sub-humans
False heaven in the clouds	Subterranean Eighth Sphere
Ungrounded dreamer	Selfish egotist
Habitual liar	Possessed by cleverness
Inflammatory diseases/insanity	Tumors, carcinomas, diabetes
Fallen beings from Saturn/Jupiter/Mars	Fallen beings from Moon/Venus/Mercury
Warmth & Light Ether—Forces of Levity	Sound & Life Ether—Forces of Gravity

Lucifer battles with mature, moral beings from Saturn, Jupiter, Mars and works on the exterior and sense organs of the human being.

Ahriman battles with mature, moral beings from Moon, Venus, Mercury through the interior organs of flesh and blood (metabolism) in the human body.

The Battle for the Soul of Humanity

Man's Life on Earth and in the Spiritual Worlds, Rudolf Steiner, Lecture V, *Luciferic and Ahrimanic Powers Wrestling for Man*, London, November 16, 1922, GA 218

"Behind Nature lies a kind of second Nature, —a spiritual, super-sensible Nature. Nature to which we are accustomed, man perceives with his senses. The super-sensible Nature that is behind, he does not perceive. It has, nevertheless, a great influence upon him.

This physical Nature that we have within us and that we perceive in our instincts and urges and passions has beneath it a kingdom of beings, who are intimately connected with man, but are really sub-human.

Thus, looking around us with the help of our senses, we behold the surface of Nature, her external appearance; and behind it we have to divine the presence of a super-sensible nature. When on the other hand we look within and perceive ourselves in our instincts and passions, then we have to divine beneath these the presence of a subsensible Nature.

The super-sensible Nature that is around us can be understood and appreciated only by one who is equipped with spiritual insight, and who is not always focusing attention, as Natural Science does to-day, on the strict laws of Nature and on what takes place within their framework.

As a matter of fact, beings live in all the various manifestations of wind and weather,—beings who are only not seen because they lack a body that is visible to the senses. The beings who live in wind and weather have a body that consists of air and warmth, a body that has in it no water—no fluidity, that is, of any kind—and no solid Earth; it consists of nothing but air and warmth. These are Luciferic beings. These beings attach great value to the moral element in the human social order. So highly do they prize it, that in their opinion it would be best for man not to have a physical body at all—not, at any rate, a body that partakes of the watery or Earthly elements. If they could have formed man in their own way, they would have made of him a moral being, pure and simple. Man would not of course in that case have had freedom, he would have been moral without being inwardly free. It is these beings wage a fearful battle in the course of the year, struggling to wrest man away from the Earth and draw him into their own sphere. They would like him to be cut off from the Earth,—a complete stranger to it. On this account they are particularly dangerous for people who are inclined to any kind of visionary idealism or vague mysticism. Such persons readily fall a prey to these beings who seek to entice man away from the Earth and endow him with a kind of Angel nature, so that under no circumstances shall he find himself tempted to be otherwise than purely moral.

Inhabiting the forces that pulsate through the encircling air in all the vagaries of wind and weather, are beings who, abhorring human freedom and desiring nothing better than its complete annihilation, want to make man a moral automaton, want to make of him indeed a kind of good Angel. And they fight hard to attain their end.

There are also beings of a contrary nature and this latter class of beings has to do with all that comes to expression in man's instinctive urges and impulses, in his desires and passions. You must not however think of them as belonging first and foremost to man. In man we can see the results of their activity. But they have their home, so to speak, right on the Earth. Only we cannot see them, for these beings too have not a body that is formed in such a way as to be visible to us. They have, in fact, a body that lives entirely in the elements of Earth and water. And their deeds are to be seen in the ebb and flow of the tides, in volcanic eruptions and in earthquakes. One who has keen spiritual perception can however see behind them a world of sub-human beings, who are under the control of the powers to which I have always given the name of the ahrimanic powers.

If one considers these luciferic and ahrimanic beings by themselves, just as they are, one cannot, you know, be angry with them. Why be angry with the luciferic beings, for instance? They want to make man into a being who is moral entirely as a matter of course. What could be better? Man would, it is true, never under their influence be free, he would be an automaton; but what they seek and desire for him can nevertheless be truthfully described as good.

Now let us see what is the aim of these other [Ahrimanic] beings, who build their strongholds immediately below the surface of the Earth, and whose activities rise up into man's metabolism,—for the phenomena we observe in the tides and less frequently in volcanic eruptions and Earthquakes are always present also in the ebb and flow in man's metabolism. The Ahrimanic beings struggle to harden man; they want to make him like themselves. Were they to be successful, man would become extremely clever in the material realm—incredibly clever and intelligent. They cannot achieve their end directly, but they aim at doing so indirectly. And their efforts, which have actually been going on for thousands of years, have in fact succeeded in producing a whole race of sub-human beings.

When a man has become a prey, during his earthly life, to the Ahrimanic powers, then these powers will be able to hold on to his instinctive nature and tear it out of him after death. There exists already on the Earth a whole population of beings who have arisen in this way. They are there, in the elements of Earth and water, a sub-human race. These earth-water beings inhabit the strata immediately below the surface of the Earth. They are beings that have been snatched out of man in the moment of death. The ahrimanic powers are waiting for the time when men will descend to incarnation and, on account of a karma that their instincts and passions have prepared for them, feel particularly drawn to certain of these beings and say to themselves: "I will not go back to the spiritual world; when I have left my physical body"—out of which, as you know, man generally goes forth to a super-sensible life—"I will incorporate myself in a subsensible being of this kind. And that will mean that I shall be able to stay on the Earth. I shall not die any more but be permanently united with the Earth. Yes, I will choose to be a sub-sensible being."

The ahrimanic beings persist in believing they will ultimately be able in this way to entice such a vast number of human beings into their own race that the Earth will one day be peopled entirely with such ahrimanic sub-human beings. By this means they hope to make the Earth itself immortal, so that the hour may never come for it to perish and be dispersed in cosmic space.

We have thus around us in our earthly environment two hosts of beings; one in the air, that wants to make man moral but to lift him away from the Earth, and then we have also, immediately below the surface of the Earth, the Ahrimanic beings who want to draw man down and fasten him permanently to the Earth.

A fearful war is waged all the time between the fire-air beings and the water-earth beings; they fight to get possession of man. And it is important that man should be aware of this war that is perpetually being waged for him; he must not be blind to it.

When man is descending from the divine spiritual world in order that he may clothe himself in a body, then it is Jahve who leads him down to Earth. The Jahve Being, who has his seat in the Moon and who leads man down to Earth, claims control in man over all that has to do with the instincts and impulses of generation. He needs helpers who will in fact see to the ordering of the whole instinctive life of man. And Jahve finds such helpers in Mercury and Venus. And it is the will and concern of the beings who have joined together in this way, to control, from Moon, Mercury and Venus, the whole flesh-and-blood nature of man. Man is by no means merely an Earthly being influences play into him from the whole great Universe.

Ahrimanic beings are doomed to look for a dwelling place just below the surface of the Earth. It is not with the fire-air beings [luciferic] alone that these water-earth beings [ahrimanic] feel themselves in opposition, but particularly also with Jahve and with the powers of Venus and Mercury. And this, notwithstanding the fact that they are themselves devoid of morality. The ahrimanic beings wage war continually on Jahve and on the Venus and Mercury powers and are determined to usurp from Jahve his rightful sovereignty. For it is owing to the rightful sovereignty of Jahve that the human race as we know it has come into existence on the Earth.

Man therefore finds himself placed right in the very midst of a conflict. On one side are ranged Jahve and his hosts, who are fighting for righteousness; on the other side the hosts of Ahriman, who, in respect of cleverness, far outstrip man, and whose concern it is utterly to repudiate man's moral nature and make him into a sheer automaton of cleverness.

In the other direction are the [luciferic] beings who incorporate themselves in air and warmth. These also, like the enemies of Jahve, are immature. And the corresponding mature beings are in their case beings who dwell on Mars, Jupiter, and Saturn. And so, we find these fire-air [luciferic] beings making sallies from their strongholds not only upon the ahrimanic powers, but upon the influences that should be continually reaching man from Mars, Jupiter, and Saturn.

Now, the influences of these more distant planets,—or rather, of their spiritual beings – are to be found particularly in the eyes, in the ears,—in short, in the sense organs of man. So that, whilst Moon and Venus exercise their influence in the interior organs of man's body, Saturn, Jupiter and Mars work on man's exterior, work in his sense organs. These beings,—Saturn beings, Jupiter beings and Mars beings—have it as their special concern to make man a real Earth man; that is to say, they want first to give him senses that are properly inserted into the human organism and that remain at its surface, and then to supply him with nerves that run from the senses and extend inwards into the organism. Saturn gives the senses, Jupiter gives their continuation in the nerves, and Mars exerts the kind of control that endows man, for example, with the faculty of speech. The whole aim and purpose of these beings is to furnish man with all that is on the surface of his body. For the senses, and the nerves too, have come about through a 'turning outside in' of the human skin.

Jupiter, Saturn, and Mars are however resisted in their activities by the [immature] fire-air beings of whom we were speaking. Here again, a furious fight goes on all the time. The fire-air beings sit fast, so to speak, in their airy strongholds and display their power and might in the fiery flashes of the lightning. They would like to make the whole of man what he should properly be on the surface only, so that the entire physical being of man should partake of the nature that is assigned only to eye and ear and nose. They would like to pour the surface of man's organism right through him, to make him all surface, so that he would do nothing but see and hear,—never eat nor drink, but only see and hear, be in fact a kind of Angel being.

The [mature] Mars, Jupiter and Saturn beings permeate what to our eyes appears mere Nature, with morality. In this manner they bring morality to man; for it is actually so, morality enters into us through the senses. When therefore the [immature] fire-air beings seek to permeate man through and through with his sense nature, it is with the intention that man, seeing nothing but what is moral, may become a moral automaton.

If we look out on the world of Nature, we can know that whatever manifests as forces in that world comes from the Mars beings, whatever manifests as natural law from the Jupiter beings, and whatever manifests as color and sound from the Saturn beings. And the fire-air beings would have man become nothing but force, law (thought), color and sound. They want man not to have a physical body at all, but to be insubstantial, rarefied; they would like him to be, as we said, an Angel being.

And so you see, whilst in external nature Moon, Mercury, Venus, Jupiter, Mars and Saturn live at peace with one another and are held in balance by the Sun, they wage a double fight for the possession of man. First of all, there is the conflict that goes on between the ahrimanic and the luciferic beings; and then secondly, the fight that is put up by the luciferic beings against the planetary forces beyond the Sun,—the Mars, Jupiter, and Saturn influences— whilst on the other hand the Ahrimanic forces are waging war on the influences that proceed from Moon, Venus and Mercury.

Let us suppose for a moment that the ahrimanic powers were victorious in the physical body of some person, victorious, that is, over the luciferic powers who try to permeate man throughout with what should by rights be only on the surface, only in the senses. The result would be that the person would succumb to illnesses producing tumors or carcinoma, or else to illnesses of the metabolism, such as diabetes. Illness is in very many cases the sole means left to the good Powers to rescue man from the fangs of Ahriman.

If on the other hand Lucifer gains a victory in a man's physical nature over the ahrimanic powers then the person concerned succumbs to illnesses of an inflammatory nature, or else to insanity.

The ahrimanic and luciferic powers, who work unceasingly with all their might for the attainment of their ends, are thus compelled to turn away sad and disappointed from beds of sickness, from hospitals and from mental asylums. These show them all too clearly that though they may continue to carry on their fight, they cannot ever be victorious.

For when the luciferic powers are victorious over the ahrimanic in the ether-body, then the person becomes a liar, he becomes a habitual liar. In that case he is obviously not moral; and so, he falls out of the world within which Lucifer would like to secure him. Instead of making him a moral automaton, Lucifer has turned him into a liar. If, on the other hand, Ahriman were to conquer, or come near to conquering the ether body, then the person would become possessed—possessed by his own cleverness.

Let us now see what can happen with the astral body. Suppose the ahrimanic powers come near to being victorious in the astral body. The person in question will in this case tend to become an out-and-out egoist. But that will mean that he, as an egoist, keeps fast hold of his instincts, and there will be no chance for Ahriman to snatch them away. So once more, Ahriman's prize escapes him. Suppose on the other hand. Lucifer nearly gains a victory. Then the person is liable to turn into a dreamer in the astral body, to become an ego-less dreamer, who is, as one says, "not in his right mind." Such things happen; it can well be that people succumb, if only for a time, to such a condition. The luciferic and ahrimanic powers are thus subject to disillusionment on Earth in many directions.

At the present time, when you cross the Threshold to the Spiritual World, you find yourself only in the midst of the terrific conflict of which we have spoken, between beings of the upper planets who have remained behind in their evolution,—immature Mars, Jupiter and Saturn beings—and beings of the lower planets who have remained behind,—immature Moon, Mercury and Venus beings. Like two armed encampments they stand facing one another; on one side, the fire-air beings,—Saturn, Jupiter and Mars beings that have failed and fallen out of their true evolution; and on the other side, facing them, the water-Earth beings,—Moon, Mercury and Venus beings who have also failed and fallen behind.

But as for man, if he can find the right relation to the Christ, then it will be given him not to despair, even in face of the despair of higher beings than himself,—beings however whose will it is to go another way than the way of the Gods to whom man belongs and to whom he should remain true throughout the further course of the Earth. At the center of these sublime God Beings is the Christ Being, who spoke to the initiates of old through the Sun disk and who speaks also to us—but now from the Earth with the help of the Sun.

When therefore we speak of Christ today, we are speaking of One who can be at our side here on Earth as our leader, guiding us out of the terrible conflict that the luciferic and ahrimanic powers are waging with one another and with the worlds of the Upper and Lower Gods."

Sorat the Sun Demon

According to Rudolf Steiner, the Sun-demon is the opposite of the Sun forces of Christ—(also called: Elohim, the Exusiai, Powers, or Spirits of Form) which reside on the Sun. As Christ works from the Divine Trinity (Father, Christ the Son, and the Holy Spirit) into physical manifestation, He uses the combined forces of the seven Elohim (the Sun and the six major planets) as His vehicle to hold His presence in our solar system. Christ's work in the hierarchy of the Elohim created the archetype that human's use as their ego, or "I Am." That is why we seek to have the higher ego of Christ live in our personal ego. The human being will eventually have three egos, the Spirit Self (our Personal Ego), the Life Spirit (the Group Ego of Christ), and the Spirit Human (the Cosmic Ego of Christ). During the Spirit Human (Atman) time of evolution, we will unite with the Sun and then go beyond the Sun to the entire Cosmos—Zodiac.

The question of Sorat's nature and mission is only lightly touched upon by Rudolf Steiner. Sorat lives on the Sun now, fighting with the forces of Christ that work through the forces of the Sun.

Sorat is technically a fallen, (retarded or laggard) Spirit of Form that stayed behind to create the opposing evil that fights with the Christ Sun forces.

Lucifer is a retarded Angel being who incarnated as a human in China between 2000-3000 B. C. in a physical body and now continues to work against humanity.

Ahriman is a retarded Archangelic being who has incarnated in our current time (Second Millennium AD) somewhere in North America and leads the spirits of materialism.

Lucifer incarnated before Christ, and Ahriman incarnates after the incarnation of Christ in Jesus of Nazareth. These two evil forces are the counterbalance for the incarnation of Christ, which was the "Turning Point of Time." There are also evil beings called **Asuras** (retarded Archai beings) who do not incarnate in a human body for they are "legion,"- many beings that do not participate in human physical incarnation.

Sorat (retarded Spirit of Form) lives on the Sun and will not incarnate in a physical body for a long time but does periodically influence evolution. Sorat lives through the expression of the Asuras who try to "eat" the ego of human beings. Sorat tries to eat the personal ego of humans through stealing aspects of the ego that humans have given up through unconscious actions and lack of morality. Sorat rules the Seven Deadly Sins that eat the human soul and spirit (pride, envy, lust, greed, gluttony, sloth, and anger). These vices, or sins, are the opposite of the Seven Heavenly Virtues that Christ instills in the ego of the human being.

In ancient Persia, Zarathustra was able to see the being of Christ descending to the Earth in the rays of the Sun before his physical incarnation as Christ Jesus at the Turning Point of Time. These living rays of life spoke to Zarathustra, and he was able to translate the rays of the Sun into gifts of Christ to help humanity. Zarathustra was given a "golden blade" to plow the Earth and transform plants and animals into the edible foods we still use today. He cross-bred the lily with the grasses of the fields to create grains and cross-bred the rose with vines and trees to create fruits; he also domesticated our "farm" animals. Zarathustra was in direct contact with Christ as He descended from the Sun to the Earth; Zarathustra called Christ, Ahura Mazda.

In our age, if you look at the Sun too long you will go blind; too much Sun will cause cancer, shingles, and many other illnesses. We also know that all life comes from the Sun when its day-forces are balanced with the night-forces of the Moon. Waking and sleeping, day and night, are the daily rhythms that rock humanity to sleep. We are not ready to stay awake all day and night—at least not yet. If you had wings and could rise up above the Earth high enough, there would be no night—just perpetual day via continuous Sunlight. If the atmosphere, with its many layers, did not blanket the Earth the Sun would cook the Earth and no life would exist. It is because the Earth rotates that we have an atmosphere at the surface of the Earth that is perfectly suited to human life. It is the great cosmic dance that harmonizes the opposites; the gift of Christ balancing gravity and levity—darkness and light.

There are four ethers that we can detect on the Earth—warmth, light, sound, and life. There is another ether called akasha that binds these four together. Five ethers create the world. But sound and life ether only have a reflection of their true nature on the Earth, under the atmosphere that covers us. The true nature of sound ether and life ether comes directly from the Sun but does not make it through the atmosphere of the Earth. Deadly cosmic rays come from the Sun that need to be filtered out in our present time, but in the future those same cosmic rays will bring nourishment because they carry the true nature of sound ether and life ether. Steiner calls the higher sound ether and life ether, the Tree of Life.

Currently, there are initiates who are more advanced than other people who can "pull down" capacities that humans will develop in the future. These individuals can rise-up through certain breath exercises and timing aligned with the five ethers, and consume the cosmic rays of the Sun that are the "unfallen" sound ether and life ether. Humanity will be able to participate in this spiritual nourishment in the future when all that we will need for life will come from the rays of the Sun and the air, light, water, and warmth that surrounds us. That time is far distant and there are very few people who can consistently gain all of their nourishment from "solar yoga" or "Sun-gazing" at this point in evolution. Usually, watching the sunrise and "breathing" in the first ether of the day is enough for most people. Others can take in much more, and some can go so far as to give up food and water altogether. These initiates are exceptions to the general rule of "moderation in all things"—including Sunlight.

In general, thankfulness and gratitude to the Sun should be our constant prayer and acknowledgement of the divine. All that we see and are, comes from the Sun. Our thoughts and nerves are simply captured Sunlight in the cave of our own body. We are little "Suns in the becoming" through the warmth we create, the light (thoughts) we shine on others, and the life we share through love. The Sun is found in the human heart and the organs that surround it are copies of the six planets. We are a solar system in miniature. We should emulate the Sun and use the Sun as our personal goal and role model. In the far future, we will unite again with the Sun, for indeed we came "out of the Sun" in the past and will "return to the Sun" in the future, but only when we can create a Sun, in miniature, in our heart.

The Nature of Sorat the Sun Demon

Every level of the celestial hierarchy has beings who have resolved to remain behind normal evolution, motivated by their own selfish desires. This process of devolution is often called evil and is mistakenly assumed to work against spiritual evolution when, in fact, without this "evil" good would have nothing to "come up against" to stimulate appropriate development. These "fallen" hierarchical beings are generally called the luciferic hosts, as described in the Christian *Bible* as the casting out of Lucifer from heaven. These "falls" from grace happen continuously and also can happen to humans as they "fall" from being truly human into animality or transhumanism. Some humans are also tempted by elemental beings to degenerate into animal, plant, and even mineral states of consciousness.

There is tremendous confusion about what Dr. Rudolf Steiner has said about the different types of evil that affect human development. Unfortunately, there are numerous "teachers" who spout Steiner's indications without adequate research and study and lead people astray. Steiner's descriptions of Lucifer, Ahriman, Asuras, and the Sun Demon Sorat have been rolled up into a ball of confusion by many who have not devoted the requisite 10-20 years of studying Steiner's opus (over 20 books and 6,000 lectures). Often, a milquetoast version or a cartoon caricature arises that is then taught to people who are just beginning to read and study Anthroposophy, and thus many mistakes are made, and nonsense is propagated as Steiner "truths." This confusion, conflation, confabulation, and nonsense has led many people to misunderstand Steiner's wisdom. In fact, leaders in the Anthroposophical Society and authors writing books for anthroposophic publishers are not being questioned about their personal interpretations of Steiner's view of evil. Due to the tremendous amount of evil in the world today, this misguidance is quite dangerous to the unwitting new student of spiritual science.

We have produced many writings on the nature of evil to try to rectify these misrepresentations, but as evil grows, so does the disinformation concerning its true nature. Many pseudo-spiritual scientists are preaching their version of the nature of Lucifer and Ahriman and ignore the evil work of the Asuras and Sorat. The question of whether the being of materialism, Ahriman, has now incarnated in a human body, as Steiner indicated, is often misunderstood. These indications are hotly debated by people who obviously have not read all that Steiner said about Ahriman. Even the human incarnation of Lucifer in China is debated and so confusing that the benefits of Steiner's wisdom is wasted on misinterpretations of partially informed people. The misdirection of "new versions" of Lucifer and Ahriman are distracting from the more deadly and permanent effects of the Asuras who "take bites out the human being's ego" that can never be restored. This attack is an invitation to the Sun Demon Sorat to leave the Sun and come to Earth to claim his kingdom prepared by the Ahriman and the Asuras.

Evil hides itself purposely to try and convince humans that evil and spiritual good do not exist at all. It is only logical that if evil exists, so does good. Unfortunately, many evil humans are happy to host the demonic intentions of the counter-evolutionary forces of the Asuras, who work directly for Sorat, not Ahriman. Materialism is the new religion of Ahriman and scientists are often possessed by ahrimanic forces and controlled by the Asuras. Scientists and doctors are actively working with evil elemental beings to create inventions that eat the soul and spirit of humans. All types of graphene oxide and polyethylene glycol have been developed by the Federal agencies that are supposed to be focused on healing, but are in fact, consciously creating killer-drugs and medical procedures that create new illnesses and iatropic death. This scientific genocide is exactly what Steiner, and other spiritual scientists, predicted will create the "War of All against All" and what we generally understand as the apocalypse, the end times. These scenarios are not supposed to happen until the Moon reunites with the Earth in approximately 6,000 years but are apparently beginning to happen now, in an attempt to destroy the divine plan.

Rudolf Steiner warned his followers numerous times that if the forces of materialism, which started around 1400 AD and came strongly to Earth around 1840, were to prevail against the forces of the spirit, the apocalypse could appear 6,000 years early and wipe out the spiritual plan for human evolution. Many have not taken this indication seriously and therefore underestimate what we have recently seen as the global plan to hand human development over to selfish, evil demons, working through humans, whose greatest desire is to end humanity all together. Being naive to these indications has led many to speculate that humanity is doing fine and in no danger. This is the biggest mistake that humanity collectively can make concerning these issues. Underestimating the power of the Asuras and Sorat leads to human extinction.

How do we counteract the overt attacks of Ahriman and Sorat? We must closely monitor the work of these demon-possessed scientists and doctors and hold them accountable for premeditated mass-murder and the willful intent to exterminate humanity. These demon-possessed individuals know clearly what they are doing but imagine that since they don't take the deadly medicines themselves, they will ultimately be the ones to inherit the world after their eugenic depopulation programs are complete. They have fallen prey to believing the "father of lies" that only the elite (who know the secret agenda) will be left to rule the world. These murderers will be wiped out also, just like those they targeted. This is the testament of evil eugenic occultism and diabolic mechanical occultism. Evil has no friends. Lucifer and Ahriman hate each other and cannot see the Christ, the Sun Hero who fights directly against Sorat. Instead, they seat Sorat on the throne of Christ in their hearts and worship his minions.

Look around the world and you will see evil death-dealing "inventions" and "medicines" being discovered every day and no one is monitoring the moral or immoral ramifications of these supposed "innovations." There are literally thousands of evil medical treatments and scientific inventions that are made to harm humans, and yet they are allowed, even though they are not "approved." Every vaccination in America, according to the drug companies own disclosures, is filled with graphene oxide and polyethylene glycol and many other carcinogens. Evil seems to not even try to hide in the modern scientific age.

Lucifer, in our time, can be found active in the astral body of humans. Taming that astral "dragon" is the same mission of an aspirant who is trying to tame his astral body. The astral body is the entire accumulation of the wisdom of the animal world rolled into the "paragon" of the animal kingdom—the human being. Lucifer would be happy if all humans devolve into animals by extinguishing higher human thinking. Lucifer infects human thinking until no life is left and human thinking becomes selfish, delusional thinking that replaces healthy human thinking. Artificial intelligence is Lucifer's delusional thinking that is working through ahrimanic anti-human machines. Basically, a lie wrapped in a conundrum.

War and hatred are inspired by Lucifer to help destroy spiritual evolution through egotism and evil thinking. Ahriman, on the other hand, is found in the etheric body of the human being as entropy, gravity, illness, old age, and death. The etheric body is levity and the source of life for the human being and the Earth. Ahriman's materialistic science is focused on gravity and leads to a cold, dark grave with no hope of an afterlife and finds its home in human feelings—cold, dead, selfish feelings. The Asuras are found outside of the human body trying to get in and destroy the eternal nature of the human ego. Thus, modern materialistic science has created substances that literally consume the eternal spirit-nature of the human being in an attempt to annihilate all humans. The Asuras were not supposed to have such power in our time, but science and medicine is ruled by ahrimanic minions who possess evil humans as the conduit for new inventions that attempt to extinguish the human spirit.

Can we stop these evil beings from bringing on the apocalypse 6,000 years early? We believe that consciousness is the most powerful tool in this battle; therefore, bringing the true nature of evil to the attention of a few aspirants may be all that is necessary to stop the disruptive plan of the evil ones. Forty-eight initiates (4 x12) becoming aware of this evil is the antidote to an accelerated timeline of human evolution that leads to the destruction of the human "I Am."

Sadly enough, two-thirds of humanity will not listen to Steiner's indications and may be lost to this diabolic plan of evil entities. Shining light on this nefarious plan is tantamount to defusing it. Evil cannot harm those who have Christ on the throne of their hearts. Ahriman and Lucifer cannot see Christ at all and don't know yet that they have already been defeated as humans accept the grace, mercy, and love of Christ that is part of the divine plan for humanity.

Rudolf Steiner on Sorat

Reading the Pictures of the Apocalypse, Rudolf Steiner, Part One, Lecture I, Munich, April 22, 1907, GA 104A

"The number 666, which in Hebrew letters spells "Sorat." Sorat is also the corresponding word in Greek. Sorat has meant "Demon of the Sun" since ancient times. Every star has its good spirit—its intelligence—and its evil spirit—its demon. The adversary of the good powers of the Sun is called Sorat. Christ was always the representative of the Sun, namely, the intelligence of the Sun. Sorat is, then, the adversary of Christ Jesus."

Reading the Pictures of the Apocalypse, Rudolf Steiner, Part Two, Lecture X, Kristiania, May 19, 1909, GA 104A

"When the seventh trumpet sounds forth a kind of blessed state will come upon humanity. Then we come to a repetition of the time when the Sun was separated from the Earth. The human being, together with the Earth, will have advanced to the time when the Sun again unites with the Earth. The Earth will pass over into what is called an astral state. Human beings able to live in the astral world will raise up the finer part of the Earth and then be united with the Sun. The portion of the Earth that has remained coarse will be united with the Moon to form a new kind of Moon. The kind of conditions prevailing during the Hyperborean age will enter in again, but at a higher stage of evolution. This is characterized by the woman clothed with the Sun and having the Moon at her feet. The beasts that rise-up out of the sea or fall from heaven also belong to this whole stream of evolution that is pictured, as if captured in a moment of time. (*Revelation* 12:1–13:10)

Zarathustra also referred to the Christ being, who has been working in the central regions of the Earth from the event of Golgotha onward. After working on the Earth from the Sun in earlier times, he has united with the Earth. It is the power of Christ that has descended from the Sun and retrieved the useful part of Earthly humanity, uniting it with the Sun again. But he has an adversary—every such being has an adversary. Christ is the good spirit, the intelligence of the Sun; the adversary is the demon of the Sun. Certain forces that are constantly working on the human astral body come forth from the demon of the Sun. This demon of the Sun is the opponent of the Christ spirit and is called Sorat. Earlier, in cabalistic sections of occultism, the custom of writing letters with numbers prevailed. The letters of the name Sorat, the demon of the Sun, have the value 666. In the picture found in *Revelation* 13:11–18, the Sun demon becomes visible.

It has two horns like a lamb. The writer of the Apocalypse describes the sign of the beast. Already at the beginning of the Apocalypse he clearly stated he was describing everything in signs and then adds: Wisdom is necessary in order to solve this riddle. In this way, the number of the Beast has been explained in occult schools by real experts who do not explain it materialistically. We hear how the worst and coarsest elements are thrown out and how the noblest, spiritualized portion of humanity remains united with the Sun. The newly spiritualized human body can then again be a temple for the soul."

The Apocalypse of St. John, Rudolf Steiner, Lecture XI, Nuremberg, June 29, 1908, GA 104

"We have then to supply the vowels and it reads: Sorath is the name of the Sun-Demon, the adversary of the Lamb. Every such spiritual being was described not only by name but also by a certain symbolic sign.

Now we must understand the writer of the Apocalypse rightly. At the very beginning he makes a remarkable statement, which is usually wrongly translated. The beginning of the Apocalypse runs, however "This is the revelation of Jesus Christ, which God gave unto him to show unto his servants things which must shortly come to pass; and he sent and signified it by his Angel unto his servant John." "Signified it." By this we must understand that he gives the important, the real content of the mystery in signs. He has put that which 666 expresses in signs. What he describes is the sign, and he describes it thus (*Revelations* 13:11): "And I saw another beast coming up out of the Earth; and he had two horns like a lamb." These are nothing else than the two strokes at the upper part of the sign, and in order to conceal this he simply calls the two strokes here "horns." It was always the case in the use of the mystery language that one uses a word in more than one sense so as to make it impossible for the uninitiated to understand without special effort.

That which he describes here: "It has two horns like a lamb," is the symbol of the Sun-demon, which in the mystery language is expressed by the word "Sorath," and this, if we convert the several letters into their numbers is expressed by the four numbers, 400, 200, 6 and 60. This is a very veiled way of expressing 666.

Thus, we see that the writer of the Apocalypse is referring to the adversary of the Lamb. When the Earth passes over into the spiritual, the forms of men appear below in such a way that they receive their old animal form. The beast with the seven heads and ten horns appears. But there also appears their seducer, the adversary of Christ, who has the great power to prevent their returning to the Sun. Man himself cannot be the adversary of Christ, he can only let slip the opportunity to take the Christ-principle into himself, through what dwells in him as false power; but there is such an adversary, the Sun-demon. This appears as soon as there is something that can become his prey. Before the prey is there, before the men are there with the seven heads and ten horns, there is nothing to lead astray, the tempter has nothing to seek there; but when men appear with such inclination, then comes the tempter, and he appears as the second beast and seduces them!

Thus, at the moment when the Earth passes over into the astral condition there appears that in man which existed in him when the Earth was still clothed with a covering of water. The human animal appears. From the water one sees the beast with seven heads and ten horns raise itself. Through this human animal having left the Earth unused, Sorath, the adversary of the Sun, the tempter, can now arise out of the Earth, through this he can approach man and tear him down with all his might into the abyss. Thus, from this time on we see a being drawing close to man, which has a fearful power! What, then, does this being do in order to lead man into the most horrible things one can think of? For man to be led into what is merely immoral, what is already known to normal man, it did not need this monster which appears as the Sun-demon. Only when that which in a good sense distinguishes the beings who bring salvation to the human race, only when spiritual eminence is turned to its opposite, only when spiritual power is placed in the service of the lower "I principle", can it bring humanity to the point when the beast represented with two horns gains power over it. The misuse of spiritual forces is connected with that seductive power of the beast with the two horns. And

we call this abuse of the spiritual power black magic, in contradistinction to
its right use, which is white magic.

Thus, through the separation of the human race there is prepared at
the same time the power to attain greater and greater spiritual conditions
on the one hand, and thereby to obtain the use of the spiritual forces, and
arrive at white magic; while on the other hand abuse of spiritual forces is a
preparation for the most fearful kind of power of the two horned beast—
black magic. Humanity will finally he divided into beings who practice white
magic and those who practice black magic. Thus, in the mystery of 666, or
Sorath, is hidden the secret of black magic; and the tempter to black magic,
that most fearful crime in the Earth evolution, with which no other crimes
can be compared, this seducer is represented by the writer of the Apocalypse
as the two-horned beast. Thus, there appears on our horizon, so to speak,
the division of humanity in the far distant future; the chosen of Christ, who
finally will be the white magicians, and the adversaries, the terrible wizards,
the black magicians who cannot escape from matter and whom the writer of
the Apocalypse describes as those who make prostitution with matter.

Hence this whole practice of black magic, the union which takes
place between man and the hardening in matter is presented to him in
the spiritual vision of the great Babylon, the community made up of
all those who carry on black magic, in the frightful marriage or rather,
unrestrained marriage, between man and the forces of prostituted matter.
And thus, in the far future we see two powers confronting each other; on
the one hand those who swell the population of the great Babylon, and on
the other hand those who rise above matter, who as human beings unite
with the principle represented as the Lamb. We see how on the one hand
the blackest ones segregate themselves in Babylon, led by all the forces
opposing the Sun, by Sorath the two-horned beast, and we see those who
have developed from the elect, who unite with Christ, or the Lamb, who
appears to them; the marriage of the Lamb on the one hand, and that of
Babylon, the descending Babylon, on the other! We see Babylon descend
into the abyss, and the elect, who have celebrated the marriage with the
Lamb, rise to the exercise of the forces of white magic.

As they not only recognize the spiritual forces but also understand how
to operate then magically, they are able to prepare what they possess in the

Earth for the next planetary incarnation, Jupiter. They sketch out the great outlines, so to speak, which Jupiter is to have. We see the preparatory forms, which are to survive as the forms of the next Earth incarnation, as Jupiter, come forth by the power of the white magicians: we see the New Jerusalem produced by white magic. But that which is described as Sorath—666—must first be expelled. That which has succumbed to the principle of the two-horned beast, and hence has hardened itself into the beast with the seven heads and ten horns, is driven forth. The power by which the Sun-genius overcomes those who are expelled, which drives them down into the abyss, is called the countenance of the Sun-genius and the countenance of the Sun-genius is Michael, who, as the representative, so to speak, of the Sun-genius, overcomes the beast with the two horns, the seducer, which is also called the great dragon. This is represented to the seer in the picture of Michael who has the key, who stands by the side of God and holds the opposing forces chained.

This is characterized in the Christian-Rosicrucian esotericism, the casting out of those who belong to 666, and the overcoming of the dragon, the seducer. Before our gaze to-day there appears that which the writer of the Apocalypse has enveloped in mystery, which one must first discover by removing the veil, and of which he says, "Here is Wisdom. Let him who hath understanding count the number of the beast" (that is, the two-horned beast); "for this number is 666."

Reading the Pictures of the Apocalypse, Rudolf Steiner, Part Two, Lecture XI, Kristiania, May 20, 1909, GA 104A

"When the Sun will have again united with the Earth, then human beings—through the fact that they will have purified their instincts, desires, and passions—will redeem the luciferic beings. The luciferic beings who do not go on to the Sun remain in their original condition. They then appear as expelled into the evil, lower astral world. This is the ancient snake, and it emerges as the first dragon. Therefore, when the Earth enters the Sun, a dragon appears. But there are yet other beings left behind: such human beings who could not prevent themselves from dropping back into animality, who remain slaves to their animal instincts. While the other human beings go to the Sun, these will form an evil power over and against the higher. These form the second monster, and the writer of the Apocalypse says in his exact fashion: The luciferic dragon appears in heaven because he comes from higher worlds; the second beast arises from the sea—this consists of the souls of animalistic human beings who have remained behind.

We have still a third vision, that of the black magicians. They do not remain stuck in animality; they develop spiritual abilities. In full consciousness they have turned away and provide a bodily incarnation for Sorat. That will be the incarnation in flesh of the demon of the Sun.

But then we see how the Earth emerges from the Sun yet again in the future. If the spiritual human beings were to remain united with the Sun forever, then the other human beings who, without guilt, had remained behind in animality would never be saved. So, these spiritualized people come forth once more and unite with what has fallen out of evolution in an attempt to save these backward souls. When the Earth began its existence as "Earth" it had to briefly repeat the Old Saturn, Old Sun, and Old Moon conditions once again. It went through recapitulations of those conditions before it became the present-day Earth. Now, when actual Earth conditions prevail, it must prophetically mirror the embodiments of Future Jupiter, Future Venus, and Future Vulcan. In this way, the Earth goes through seven states during its actual Earth condition. These states are usually called "rounds." During the prophetically mirrored Jupiter state, the Earth will actually unite with the Sun. On this Future Jupiter-Earth all the great cultural ages will appear again—with the seven intervals between them—but they will be far less sharply delineated. On this Future Jupiter-Earth, many beings still have the possibility of being saved, even the black magicians.

This will also be the case on the Future Venus-Earth, when we have a sixth planetary interval. Here also the beings that have remained behind will stubbornly struggle against help; but this Future Venus-Earth will at last be decisive.

Then, on the Future Vulcan-Earth, nothing more can be saved. On the Future Venus-Earth the last moment for salvation has come in the last subepoch. That is why the ancient cabalists formed the word "Sorat," because the number 666 is contained within it. That is also the number of those human beings who, out of their own cunning free will, have become black magicians by placing spiritual forces in the service of their own egotism.

The first dragon is not a human being. It came out of the spiritual world. The second dragon is ascribed to animalistic nature but in a fundamental sense the *Bible* ascribes this number of the third group to human beings. So, the number 666 is not a sign of the beast but a human number.

The Apocalypse is an outline of the whole of evolution. Future Venus-Earth is portrayed to clairvoyant sight in such a way that there is not much hope for those left behind. Human powers at that time will not be capable of very much. That is why everything appears so desolate, and the worst vices will reign there in the most depraved ways. They must be expelled during the Venus state of the Earth. On the Future Jupiter-Earth there are still many, many who will allow themselves to be saved and who will unite with the Sun.

But during the Future Venus-Earth evil must be overcome and driven into the abyss; that is the "Fall of Babylon." (Revelations 17:18) The people who have been saved can develop themselves further to a new Sun state. What has been cleansed and purified will arise for the Future Vulcan-Earth.

Human beings today are already creative on the Earth. They can force the lifeless forces of nature to serve them. They can build cathedrals and they can sculpt marble. Today they are masters of lifeless nature. Even though Raphael's paintings of the Madonna are falling to dust, even though the external physical world is passing away, what the human being achieves in terms of art during the evolution of the Earth will one day be resurrected in a different form. The crystals we see today were once forms worked out by human beings during the Old Moon embodiment of the Earth, in a way similar to how we create and form artistically today. What the spirits once achieved in infinite ages of time now grows out of the Earth; today it rises-up. So, too, the matter of Raphael's Madonnas will also rise-up. In the distant future, everything that human beings now create will rise again with the brightness of crystals. The place that humanity has prepared and will find waiting is called the "New Jerusalem" by the writer of the Apocalypse. A new world will arise, inhabitable by human beings who will have achieved the requisite state of maturity. In a new state, in the Future Jupiter existence, they will find the place where, out of love and out of human work, peace will reign."

Michaelic Verse
by Rudolf Steiner

We must eradicate from the soul all fear and terror of
what comes toward us out of the future.
We must acquire serenity in all feelings and sensations about the future.
We must look forward with absolute equanimity to all that may come,
and we must think only that whatever comes is given to us
by a world direction full of wisdom.
This is what we have to learn in our times.
To live out of pure trust in the ever-present help of the spiritual world.
Surely nothing else will do if our courage is not to fail us.
Let us properly discipline our will, and let us seek
the inner awakening every morning and every evening.

BIBLIOGRAPHY

- Gabriel, Douglas. *Goddess Meditations*. Trinosophia Press, 1994.

- Gabriel, Douglas. *The Eternal Curriculum for Wisdom Children: Intuitive Learning and the Etheric Body*, Our Spirit, 2017.

- Gabriel, Douglas. *The Eternal Ethers A Theory of Everything*. Our Spirit, 2018

- Gabriel, Douglas. *The Queens of the Grail*. Our Spirit, 2019

- Gabriel, Douglas. *The Spirit of Childhood*. Trinosophia Press, 1993.

- Gabriel, Tyla. *The Gospel of Sophia: The Biographies of the Divine Feminine Trinity (Volume 1)*, Our Spirit, 2014.

- Gabriel, Tyla. *The Gospel of Sophia: A Modern Path of Initiation (Volume 2)*, Our Spirit, 2015.

- Gabriel, Tyla and Douglas. *The Gospel of Sophia: Sophia Christos Initiation (Volume 3)*, Our Spirit, 2016.

- Steiner, Rudolf. *Ancient Myths: Their Meaning and Connection with Evolution*. Steiner Book Center, 1971.

- Steiner, Rudolf. *Between Death and Rebirth*, November 1912–April 1913, Rudolf Steiner Press, London, 1930. GA 141

- Steiner, Rudolf. *Christ and the Spiritual World: The Search for the Holy Grail*. Rudolf Steiner Press, London, 1963.

- Steiner, Rudolf. *Death as a Metamorphosis of Life, The Dead Are With Us*, Nuremberg, February 10, 1918, GA 182

- Steiner, Rudolf. *Foundations of Esotericism*. Rudolf Steiner Press, London, 1983.

- Steiner, Rudolf. *Knowledge of the Higher Worlds*, Rudolf Steiner Press, London, 1971.

- Steiner, Rudolf. *Isis Mary Sophia: Her Mission and Ours*. Steiner Books, 2003.

- Steiner, Rudolf. *Man as a Being of Sense and Perception*. Steiner Book Center, Vancouver, 1981.

- Steiner, Rudolf. *Man as Symphony of the Creative Word*. Rudolf Steiner Publishing, London, 1978.

- Steiner, Rudolf. *Occult Science*. Anthroposophic Press, NY, 1972.

- Steiner, Rudolf. *The Philosophy of Spiritual Activity*. Anthroposophic Press, NY, 1972.

- Steiner, Rudolf. *Rosicrucian Esotericism*. Anthroposophic Press, NY, 1978.

- Steiner, Rudolf. *Rosicrucian Wisdom: An Introduction*. Rudolf Steiner Press, London, 2000. GA 425

- Steiner, Rudolf. *The Bridge between Universal Spirituality and the Physical Constitution of Man*. Anthroposophic Press, NY, 1958.

- Steiner, Rudolf. *The Evolution of Consciousness*. Rudolf Steiner Press, London, 1926.

- Steiner, Rudolf. *The Goddess from Natura to the Divine Sophia*. Sophia Books, 2001.

- Steiner, Rudolf. *The Holy Grail from the Works of Rudolf Steiner*, Compiled by Steven Roboz. Steiner Book Center, North Vancouver, 1984.

- Steiner, Rudolf. *The Influence of Spiritual Beings Upon Man*. Anthroposophic Press, NY, 1971.

- Steiner, Rudolf. *Life Between Death and Rebirth The active connection between the living and the dead*, Anthroposophic Press, 1968. GA 141

- Steiner, Rudolf. *Living and the Dead*. Anthroposophic Press, New York, 1960. GA 140

- Steiner, Rudolf. *Man's Life on Earth and in the Spiritual World*, Anthroposophic Press, New York, 1922. GA 211, 124, 218

- Steiner, Rudolf. *Occult Research into Life Between Death and a New Birth.* Anthroposophic Press, 1949. GA 140

- Steiner, Rudolf. *The Mystery of Death.* 1915. Rudolf-Steiner-Verlag, 1967. GA 159

- Steiner, Rudolf. *The Reappearance of Christ in the Etheric.* Anthroposophic Press, NY, 1983.

- Steiner, Rudolf. *The Risen Christ and the Etheric Christ.* Rudolf Steiner Press, London, 1969.

- Steiner, Rudolf. *The Search for the New Isis the Divine Sophia.* Mercury Press, N.Y., 1983.

- Steiner, Rudolf. *The Spiritual Hierarchies and the Physical World.*Anthroposophic Press, N.Y., 1996.

- Steiner, Rudolf. *The Study of Man.* Rudolf Steiner Press, London, 1971.

- Steiner, Rudolf. *The Tree of Life and the Tree of Knowledge.* Mercury Press, NY, 2006.

- Steiner, Rudolf. *The True Nature of the Second Coming.* Rudolf Steiner Press, London, 1971.

- Steiner, Rudolf. *Theosophy.* Anthroposophic Press, New York, 1986.

- Steiner, Rudolf. *Wonders of the World, Ordeals of the Soul, Revelations of the Spirit.* Anthroposophic Press.

- Steiner, Rudolf. *World History in Light of Anthroposophy.* Anthroposophic Press.

- Wachsmuth, Guenther. *Reincarnation as a Phenomenon of Metamorphosis,* Philosophic-Anthroposophic Press, Dornach, 1937.

- Wachsmuth, Guenther. *The Life and Work of Rudolf Steiner From the Turn of the Century to His Death.* Whittier Books, New York, 1955.

RUDOLF STEINER

Rudolf Steiner was born on the 27th of February 1861 in Kraljevec, in the former Kingdom of Hungary, now Croatia. He studied at the College of Technology in Vienna and obtained his doctorate at the University of Rostock with a dissertation on Theory of Knowledge, which concluded with the sentence: "The most important problem of human thinking is this: to understand the human being as a free personality, whose very foundation is himself."

He exchanged views widely with the personalities involved in the cultural life and arts of his time. However, unlike them, he experienced the spiritual realm as the other side of reality. He gained access through exploration of consciousness using the same method as the natural scientist uses for the visible world in his external research. This widened perspective enabled him to give significant impulses in many areas such as art, pedagogy, curative education, medicine, agriculture, architecture, economics, and social sciences, aiming towards the spiritual renewal of civilization.

He gave his movement the name of "Anthroposophy" (the wisdom of humanity) after separating from the German section of the Theosophical Society, where he had acted as a general secretary. He then founded the Anthroposophical Society in 1913, which formed its center with the construction of the First Goetheanum in Dornach, Switzerland. Rudolf Steiner died on 30th March 1925 in Dornach. His literary work is made up of numerous books, transcripts, and approximately 6000 lectures which have for the most part been edited and published in the Complete Works Edition.

Steiner's basic books, which were previously a prerequisite to gaining access to his lectures, are: *Theosophy, The Philosophy of Freedom, How to Know Higher Worlds, Christianity as a Mystical Fact,* and *Occult Science.*

THE AUTHOR,
DR. DOUGLAS GABRIEL

Dr. Gabriel is a retired superintendent of schools and professor of education who has worked with schools and organizations throughout the world. He has authored many books ranging from teacher training manuals to philosophical/spiritual works on the nature of the divine feminine. He was a Waldorf class teacher and administrator at the Detroit Waldorf School and taught courses at Mercy College, the University of Detroit, and Wayne State University for decades. He then became the Headmaster of a Waldorf School in Hawaii and taught at the University of Hawaii, Hilo. He was a leader in the development of charter schools in Michigan and helped found the first Waldorf School in the Detroit Public School system and the first charter Waldorf School in Michigan.

Gabriel received his first degree in religious formation at the same time as an associate degree in computer science in 1972. This odd mixture of technology and religion continued throughout his life. He was drafted into and served in the Army Security Agency (NSA) where he was a cryptologist and systems analyst in signal intelligence, earning him a degree in signal broadcasting. After military service, he entered the Catholic Church again as a Trappist monk and later as a Jesuit priest where he earned PhD's in philosophy and comparative religion, and a Doctor of Divinity. As a Jesuit priest, he came to Detroit and earned a BA in anthroposophical studies and history and a MA in school administration. Gabriel left the priesthood and became a Waldorf class teacher and administrator in Detroit and later in Hilo, Hawaii.

Douglas has been a sought-after lecturer and consultant to schools and businesses throughout the world and in 1982 he founded the Waldorf Educational Foundation that provides funding for the publication of educational books. He has raised a great deal of money for Waldorf schools and institutions that continue to develop the teachings of Dr. Rudolf Steiner. Douglas is now retired but continues to write a variety of books, including a novel and a science fiction thriller. He has four children, who keep him busy and active and a wife who is always striving towards the spirit through creating an "art of life." She is the author of the *Gospel of Sophia* trilogy.

The Gabriels' articles, blogs, and videos can currently be found at:

OurSpirit.com
Neoanthroposphy.com
GospelofSophia.com
EternalCurriculum.com

TRANSLATOR NOTE

The Rudolf Steiner quotes in this book can be found, in most cases, in their full-length and in context, through the Rudolf Steiner Archives by an Internet search of the references provided. We present the quoted selections of Steiner from a free rendered translation of the original while utilizing comparisons of numerous German to English translations that are available from a variety of publishers and other sources. In some cases, the quoted selections may be condensed and partially summarized using the same, or similar in meaning, words found in the original. Brackets are used to insert [from the author] clarifying details or anthroposophical nomenclature and spiritual scientific terms.

We chose to use GA (Gesamtausgabe—collected edition) numbers to reference Steiner's works instead of CW (Collected Works), which is often used in English editions. Some books in the series, *From the Works of Rudolf Steiner,* have consciously chosen to use a predominance of Steiner quotes to drive the presentation of the themes rather than personal remarks and commentary.

We feel that Steiner's descriptions should not be truncated but need to be translated into an easily read format for the English-speaking reader, especially for those new to Anthroposophy. We recommend that serious aspirants read the entire lecture, or chapter, from which the Steiner quotation was taken, because nothing can replace Steiner's original words or the mood in which they were delivered. The style of speaking and writing has changed dramatically over the last century and needs updating in style and presentation to translate into a useful tool for spiritual study in modern times. The series, *From the Works of Rudolf Steiner* intends to present numerous "study guides" for the beginning aspirant, and the initiate, in a format that helps support the spiritual scientific research of the reader.

Printed in Great Britain
by Amazon

47876429R00106